VOICES OFFSTAGE

By the Author

THE GREEN PASTURES

THE FARMER TAKES A WIFE
(*collaboration with Frank B. Elser*)

THE WISDOM TOOTH

HUNTER'S MOON

THE PORTABLE YENBERRY

THE FLOWERS OF VIRTUE

With George Kaufman

DULCY

MERTON OF THE MOVIES

BEGGAR ON HORSEBACK

TO THE LADIES

HELEN OF TROY, NEW YORK

BE YOURSELF

VOICES OFFSTAGE
A BOOK OF MEMOIRS
By *Marc Connelly*

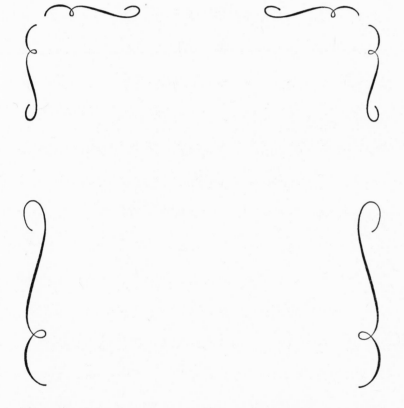

Holt, Rinehart & Winston, Inc.

Chicago · New York · San Francisco

9 2
C 9523 c

Library of Congress Catalog Card Number: 68-12204

FIRST EDITION

d

8684755
Printed in the United States of America

To the memory of Lloyd Lewis

Contents

SIXTEEN PAGES OF BLACK AND WHITE PHOTOGRAPHS
FOLLOW PAGE 150

VOICES OFFSTAGE

1

A Curtain Rises

ONE DAY when the nineteenth century was drawing to a close, my father pinned a celluloid button on my jacket. He told me that the words on it were "Boost Mc-Keesport—The Tube City!" McKeesport was my home, and I do not believe that any of my fellow residents were temperamentally more disposed to speak well of it than I. But because I was a very small boy, I was ignorant of those merits of our town that my father, a founder of its Booster Club, was prepared to communicate to any listener. I could not boast that McKeesport, Pennsylvania, the Home of the National Tube Works, outstripped the rest of the world in the production of iron pipe, was the fastest-growing city in the Monongahela Valley, and might one day be as big as Pittsburgh, fifteen miles away. I willingly wore the button, but except for inviting all I met to look at it, I took no part in stimulating McKeesport's growth.

Privately, I had not the faintest concern about the city's magnificent future. I was highly satisfied with its glorious present. By my standards McKeesport was a metropolis unlimited in area and population. Pittsburgh was only a nebulous place that people went to on the trains that arrived and departed, usually under my personal supervision, several times a day at the B. & O. depot across the street from where I lived. It was rewarding to see travelers getting on and off. And there was always the possibil-

I

ity that if I waved my hand at a conductor he would lift his in the fraternal response to another railroad man's salute.

The passenger trains were not the only entertainment the railroad provided. A block away, the tracks crossed Fifth Avenue, our busiest thoroughfare, and when long freight trains stopped to shift cars, it paid to dash down there and, as the traffic block became prolonged, watch people get mad and carry on. Later, many a citizen, on being recognized by a strangely quiet group of little boys, wondered what made them suddenly shriek at one another, fling their arms about in mock fits of rage, then suddenly stop, filled with uncontrollable merriment. McKeesport was a fine place in which to be six years old.

My home was the Hotel White, where I lived with my parents. The reason we lived there was clarified for me when my friend Murray Miller, the day clerk, explained the meaning of "P. J. Connelly, Prop." on the hotel letterhead. I was aware that P. J. Connelly was my father, but theretofore I had accepted the deference shown him by the staff as part of a natural order of things which included his authority over me.

We lived in McKeesport partly because my father's parents, his married sisters, and numerous other relatives were in nearby communities. My father had been born in Pittsburgh. When he was twenty, friends and relatives encouraged him to exploit his pleasing bass-baritone voice professionally. Armed with letters of recommendation from former teachers and several unqualified eulogies from admirers who did not reveal that they were also affectionate aunts and cousins, he presented himself to the manager of a touring stock company. The manager listened to my

2

father's singing and to one or two dramatic recitations. Because the company needed a young man to do odd jobs, my father was hired and an hour later found himself distributing handbills. By the time the troupe left town, he had proved himself generally useful and was taken along.

The company prospered. Within a few months my father was doing many of the managerial chores, playing small parts, and performing in the olio—the between-the-acts entertainment, in which members of the cast showed their versatility by singing, dancing, and exchanging banter. After a year the company disbanded in New York. My father learned that the fabulous Steele MacKaye, the dramatist, painter, lecturer at Harvard and Cornell, actor, and inventor (he had recently initiated overhead stage lighting), and the most powerful influence in the American theater, was interviewing promising newcomers. My father saw him and got a job as assistant manager of the Lyceum, on Fourth Avenue at Twenty-third Street, one of the three New York theaters MacKaye had founded. The theater changed ownership a year or so later, and my father resumed his career as an actor. In 1886 he was playing juvenile leads in a resident repertory company in Boston.

One morning late in that year, Marcus Carlon Cook, an affluent merchant, was enjoying his breakfast with unusual zest in his residence on Beacon Hill and reading the comment of the *Transcript* on the election of his friend and colleague in the Massachusetts Legislature, Henry Cabot Lodge, to the House of Representatives. Presently, Mr. Cook's wife entered the room with another announcement: their eighteen-year-old daughter, Mabel, would not be breakfasting with them that morning. The opening lines of a letter she had left for them on a dressing table stated that she had decided to elope with Joseph. For a moment, the stunned Cooks could not identify Joseph, but the succeeding lines of the letter made his identity excruciatingly obvious. He was That Actor.

Months before, Patrick Joseph Connelly had appeared at teatime, on Mabel's invitation. After his second call within forty-eight hours, Mabel had been told that despite a proper introduction in a friend's house, he was not welcome in her home. Any performer on the stage, particularly one whose parents had been Irish immigrants, was hardly a desirable acquaintance.

Mabel's letter provided one meager grain of comfort: she was not joining the Roman Catholic Church; Joseph had no objection to her remaining an Episcopalian.

The elopers left Boston immediately. For a time, the Cooks wrote no replies to the affectionate letters Mabel sent from different inland cities. Their chilled affection grew icy when Mabel wrote that she herself was acting. But, eventually, theatrical reviews clipped from newspapers in several large cities prompted a reappraisal of the runaway. A girl who could elicit such wide respect for her portrayal of the title role in *Hazel Kirke* obviously had artistic genius her parents had never suspected. And if her husband, now the manager of the company she was in, was as devoted as every letter she wrote implied, perhaps they had been hasty in their first judgment of him.

In Pittsburgh, the undiminished love of all the Connellys for Patrick Joseph assuaged the pain of his marriage to a non-Catholic. At the end of the theatrical season the

4

young couple was welcomed when they made filial visits
to Pittsburgh and Boston.

My parents' stage careers ended abruptly the following year in Duluth. They were again on tour and had their
three-month-old daughter with them. The baby died suddenly of pneumonia. Their anguish was intensified by self-
reproach for having subjected her to the hazards of travel.
They wanted another child, so they quit the stage and settled in McKeesport. I was born there about a year later.

I was very young when my father bought the Hotel
White, and I have only a few wispy memories of my existence prior to our moving there. But by the time I became
the owner of the Booster Club button, fumbling but increasingly frequent impulses to relate thought to experience, were giving me highly personal opinions. These
early views of life were often askew and out of focus. The
world, for all I knew, automatically closed up shop when I
went to bed. That there might be any after-hours activity
never entered a mind too busy establishing its own existence to consider the doings of other people. But one night
I learned that life had much to offer after 8 P.M.

It was probably about seven when the adventure
began. To my bewilderment, I found myself donning my
best day clothes instead of my nightgown. I heard my
father anxiously declaring that we must hurry, and my
mother told me we were going to Pittsburgh. I might also
have been told the reason for our journey, but if so, I did
not listen. The knowledge that I was not in bed and that
we were going on a train was so delicious that at the moment I had no appetite for other considerations. In the
booming confusion of childhood, trifles are more impressive than occasions. I vaguely remember the train trip and

a subsequent ride in a horse-drawn cab that took us to our destination.

We entered a strange building. In a room even larger than the lobby of the Hotel White, a man stood beside a door, his fingers pressed to his lips, cautioning silence. My father whispered, "Has it been up long?"

"About half an hour," the man replied.

We went through the door and up a flight of stairs to a small cluster of empty chairs that stood in near darkness. The dim light and the murmur of subdued voices some-where near us suggested that another of my many Con-nelly relatives had died. (I had recently attended the fu-neral services of my father's mother in a Catholic church. The difference between its dusky interior and the compar-ative brightness of St. Stephen's Protestant Episcopal Church in McKeesport had impressed me.) I asked who had died. My mother whispered that no one was dead and bade me sit quietly beside her.

The position of my chair enabled me to peer over a plush-covered balustrade that curved around us. On our right was a colossal painting that stretched from a remote ceiling to the floor. It was too dimly lit for me to see all its details, but at the bottom there was a soft glow of hidden lights. In the semidarkness, I could make out the forms of people down below us and others in a sort of choir loft suspended in the air on my left. Seemingly, my parents and I were in something like the pulpit in which the Cath-olic priest had stood when he spoke to God about my grandmother. As my eyes grew accustomed to the light, I could see that the people sitting below us were conducting themselves much more informally than did the congrega-tion on Sundays in St. Stephen's. Nor were the pews in

6

which they sat like any I had seen. Instead of forming straight lines, they nestled one behind the other in arcs. Surveying the choir loft, I saw that it extended from wall to wall and that its occupants—not one of whom wore choir vestments—filled all the embanked rows of seats, which receded up into complete darkness. I half-expected a Catholic priest, or the Reverend George F. Rosenmüller of St. Stephen's, to appear and conduct whatever formalities were imminent.

I did not await either the clergy or the ritual with any eagerness. For several months I had been a member of St. Stephen's choir and I had grown blasé about the parts of the service in which I had nothing to do but sit still. Hence, during the tedious stretches on Sunday mornings, I studied members of the congregation. (Old Mrs. Harper, for instance, was a Daughter of the King. Dr. Rosenmüller, a fairly reliable informant, had once told me that the impressive plaque near the vestry door listed the names of several ladies of the parish who were Daughters of the King. Mrs. Harper was the only one I knew personally, and it was worthwhile to study her big, round body and her little black hat and ponder that, while she looked like almost anybody and sold candy in her little store up on Huey Street, she was also a princess whose father had a kingdom somewhere. It was not until after I had been admitted to the Junior Brotherhood of St. Andrew, at the age of ten, that I learned that the Daughters of the King were members of an Episcopalian women's society.)

I was still gaping at the strangers about us when those who had been chatting with inappropriate frivolity suddenly softened their voices. Their faces were bathed in a new, warm light. I turned my head toward its source, and found that the gigantic painting had disappeared completely. I was staring at a bakery—a large, cheerful-looking bakery, framed in darkness. It was open for business and bustling with activity. I recognized the bakers by their hats and aprons, though their short pants and colored stockings were unfamiliar. The clothes of the few women in the shop were peculiar but easily ignored: I knew that ladies everywhere wore anything they wanted to at any time.

The male customers, however, differed from any adults I had ever met. Almost all wore swords that resembled those our McKeesport soldiers had held up for us to admire as they marched past the reviewing stand after setting Cuba free. The high boots the customers strode about in implied that they might be fishermen, but it was hard to picture them wading after pickerel in the Monongahela dressed in those fancy long coats and big plumed hats, which they had obviously borrowed from their wives. However, no one in the bakery made fun of them, and because there were other oddities to observe, I soon accommodated myself to their appearance.

I noticed in the rear of the bakery two large windows that looked out on a sunny street. I recalled that it had been nighttime when my parents and I left the cab a few minutes previously, but I was not disconcerted. I accepted the rearrangement of time as a mildly noteworthy but no doubt common local practice.

The bakery filled with more customers. One of them caught and held my attention. He was tall and dashing and did not seem to mind having an abnormally long nose. Nor did those about him pay any attention to his nose. They listened to everything he had to say. Now and then, some of the people below me and in the choir loft laughed while he was speaking. As nothing being said in the bakery had meaning for me, I could only suspect that his nose had something to do with the mirth, which he disregarded except when, occasionally, he had to stop talking with his friends until the noisy hilarity of the people in the pews died down.

Soon I had attention for no one but him. My mother's periodic reminders not to fidget ceased. The man was hypnotically engrossing as he strode about defying the world, a little ridiculous with that long nose, yet at the same time brave and noble.

Then, my enchantment was abruptly broken by a horrifying convulsion of nature. Though I had been undisturbed by a twelve-hour displacement of the sun, I now quailed at what was happening before my eyes. A wall was descending, descending from nowhere, and before anybody could lift a finger in self-protection, it had obliterated the bakery and every soul in it. I turned to my father for an explanation. He and my mother had lost their wits and were clapping their hands. The next moment an explosion of sound struck me from behind. I spun around and leaned over the rail of our pulpit. Everyone on our side of the wall, the people below, and those in the choir loft were all clapping. Some had begun to cheer. Every second, the wave of hysteria grew wilder. I was witnessing conduct even more unbridled than one saw on Friday afternoons when the Market Street Public School let out. Here was something that baffled understanding: a multitude of grownups were wildly acclaiming an appalling disaster.

I turned back to my father, confused and a little

frightened. "Look at the stage," he said, pointing to where the bakery had been. I looked. Incredibly, the wall was rising from the ground. As it did, the bakery reappeared, undamaged, with everybody who had been in it standing there without a scratch. I, too, now joined the hubbub, my own clamor prompted solely by the miraculous return of the bakery.

My quick adjustability to any circumstance made the second descent of the wall less terrifying, and the wall became only an irritating nuisance when it persisted in first hiding the bakery, then soaring away again as the din continued. At last, during one of its withdrawals, my long-nosed idol magically arrested its return by holding up his hand. His former companions had now all run away, leaving him alone.

He stepped to the forward edge of the bakery and looked about at the noisemakers. Everyone quieted down. I thought he was going to scold us. His searching eyes momentarily glanced in my direction, and I half-expected to hear a reproof addressed directly to me. Instead, as soon as we were all silent he smiled and, in a voice much gentler than the one he had been using before, said he was not there merely to thank us for approving his efforts. He hoped we were going to be generous enough to do something he had never asked of an audience before and probably never would again. He said it might be a test of our endurance. Among us was an old friend of his, whom he had met shortly after coming to America from England many years before. His friend had wanted to witness tonight's performance but had arrived too late to see it begin. This was the test: How many of us were willing to allow him and his company to replay the part his friend had missed?

There were little gasps of surprise and delight, followed by a great thunderclap of laughter and applause. I stood up with everyone else. We passed the test unanimously.

Since then, the stage and much of its mechanics have become familiar to me. What I have learned has substantiated my early feeling that going to the theater is like going to an unusual church, where the spirit is nourished in mysterious ways, and pure magic may occur at any moment. It is also pleasant to recall that that feeling first stirred my mind the night Richard Mansfield twice played Act I of *Cyrano de Bergerac* for my father because of a belated B.&O. train from McKeesport.

McKeesport, Fun City

ONE DAY WHEN I was seven I discovered that my father was the wittiest man in the world. Our visits to my aunts, uncles, and cousins in the vicinity of McKeesport were highlighted by lavish family dinners. I was as eager to eat as any child at the table, but my appetite was invariably keener for the drollery my father might provide at the end of the meal. Although an inexperienced judge of humor, I was appreciative enough to know that the joke my father might be moved to tell was one that could not be surpassed. It was The King of Jokes. The first time I heard it I had to get up from my chair and stamp my foot several times in a delirium of mirth which laughter alone could not fully relieve. Its lightning impact lost no force by repetition.

The core of the joke lay in the diners' awareness that, course after course, my father had consumed with relish everything set before him. If, after his second helping of dessert and third cup of coffee I saw him smiling with repletion, I would begin to burn with a tantalizing fever of expectancy. When he patted his stomach with both hands and gained everyone's attention by an audible sigh of satisfaction, I knew The Joke Supreme was on its way to utterance. Conversation halted and all eyes turned to my father. Aware that that grave look on his face was intended to make everyone think he was about to speak solemnly, I had to clench my fists and look away to keep the welling laughter from strangling me.

"Well," my father would say with grave thoughtfulness, "thank God for that little bite. Many a man might have had to make a meal of it."

I never measured how much hilarity swept through the rest of the audience. I was blind to everything but the dazzling brilliance of my first after-dinner speaker.

When I grew up I wondered whether there might have been a purpose behind The Joke I did not detect. Although my aunts and uncles loved my father dearly, I doubt they would have tolerated the same witticism as many times as I seem to remember its being told. Of course, actually it might have been repeated only once or twice, and before new listeners; when you're young you don't number delights. What seems more likely is that its retelling was part of a conspiracy, the sole reason for which was the joy some grown-ups had in seeing a small boy laugh.

I could not have been much more than seven when I had a memorable experience. Because I was a tireless explorer, ready to open any unlocked door in my father's hotel, restraints running from stern reprovals to effective spankings made all but the family living quarters out of bounds. One morning my father offered me a surprising privilege. For several days posters on billboards and the sides of buildings had heralded the coming of a circus. I had gazed on them with awe. There were thrilling pictures of fierce Russian cossacks brandishing swords as they urged their wild-eyed horses toward the onlookers. Others

showed a careening stagecoach loaded with horrified passengers, all in immediate danger of being tomahawked by
bloodthirsty Indian horsemen, their only hope a troop of
U.S. Cavalry way off in the distance. Less frightening, but
as engrossing, were pictures of a lady in a buckskin suit
who, while riding a galloping mustang, was shattering
small glass balls overhead with her rifle. Circled in the
corner of every poster was another picture, that of a man
with flowing locks, a big white mustache and a pointed
beard. He sat, completely at ease, on a rearing horse, holding his wide-brimmed hat high in the air, proudly ac-
knowledging the homage of the world.

The circus was much on my mind. It had given its
first performance the day before, and I had been told that
if I was a good boy I would see it that afternoon. I listened
with close attention to my father's words.

"How would you like to be a waiter this morning?"

I said I would.

"All right, then. Take this glass of grape juice up to
room 105. Be sure to knock before you go in."

Never was a tray carried with more care. I knocked
on the door of 105. A man's voice bade me to come in.
Skillfully balancing the tray, I entered. With my eyes on
the glass, I carried it safely to a table.

"Thank you very much, young man," said the voice.
"Come over here so I can congratulate you."

I looked at the speaker. He was sitting up in bed smiling. I recognized the flowing white mustache and pointed
beard and did not have to be told that the keen blue eyes
were those of the Greatest Indian Scout in the Whole
World. If you ever meet me, I may allow you to shake the
hand that shook the hand of Buffalo Bill.

14

About the same time, my first work as an author appeared in print. Inspiration usually came to me after I had been tucked in bed and begun to think about our war with Spain. I would call out to my amanuensis, my mother, who would arrive like any efficient secretary with paper and pencil to take down my dictation. The completed work having received parental admiration, the editor of the McKeesport *Daily News*, a family friend, would be given the privilege of publishing it. A major effort, commemorating the capture of the Philippine naval base at Cavite is here reprinted in its entirety:

> When Dewey sailed into Manila Bay
> He chased those old Spaniards away.

With the end of the war, I enlarged my field of creative expression. I became an actor, author, director, producing manager, and proprietor of a theater, the Marcus Connelly Opera House. It was on the second floor of the Hotel White and when not in operation was part of our living room. My plays were a free form of *commedia dell'arte*, mostly improvised during their performance. The chairs for the audience were often vacated temporarily when their occupants were needed for roles on the stage. I was now learning to read, and virtually everything that engaged my mind was grist for the dramatic mill. One of my plays dealt with a recent jailbreak in Pittsburgh by the notorious Biddle brothers. I created several roles, portraying, among others, the older of the Biddles and Mrs. Kate Soffel, the wife of the superintendent of the Western Pennsylvania Penitentiary. She was stuck on one of the brothers and helped the getaway. In a tense scene between

15

Mr. and Mrs. Soffel I was also able to play Mr. Soffel by having an actress in my company kindly take over my role of his wife. One theatrical season was highlighted and terminated by a melodrama based on a newpaper account of a disaster at sea. The climax of the play's single presentation was reached when a ship's mainsail, recently a bed sheet in the hotel linen closet, blazed with thrilling effectiveness.

My first collaboration as a writer occurred when I was nine. Will Marion Cook, a well-known composer of popular music, had come to McKeesport to conduct the orchestra of his new musical show *Bon Bon Buddy* in White's Opera House, our "legitimate" theatre. Mr. Cook, on learning I was a poet—undoubtedly from me—suggested that I write the lyrics of a song, which he promised to set to music. I do not remember the drivel he somehow managed to fit to a tune, but for weeks afterward I sang it to anyone unable to escape. It did not occur to me then, that I had become a songwriter only because my father had made clear to Mr. Cook and his stars, Bert Williams and George Walker, all of whom were Negroes, that Negro artists were welcomed guests at the Hotel White.

When I was twelve you couldn't have convinced me that McKeesport was not the entertainment capital of the world and an endless festival of fun. In the spring and summer there were the circuses. Because McKeesport was a big city ("We have a population of thirty-six thousand though the census only gives us twenty-eight."—*P. J. Connelly to someone within earshot of his son*), we were visited annually by the big three-ring aggregations of Adam Forepaugh, Sells-Floto, Barnum and Bailey, and the Ringling Brothers as well as smaller assemblages. My good friend Buffalo Bill was not the only former Indian fighter to come every year. There was Major Gordon R. Lillie, who called himself Pawnee Bill. His entertainment was not quite as splendid as Buffalo Bill's, but that he, too, had been a brave scout was certified by his long locks, widespread mustache, and fine goatee.

Summers always brought carnivals to town. Each lasted a week and was sponsored by the Elks, the Eagles, the McKeesport Fire Department, or other organizations. They provided noisier and more dazzling diversions than were available at Kennywood, Calhoun, Olympia, or Versailles parks, suburban recreation grounds operated by the street-car companies.

It was exciting to stroll about the carnival grounds. If I had the necessary dimes, I would buy wonderful examples of the glass-blower's art—swans I had seen created before my eyes, or glasses of wine which, no matter how you tipped them, held their contents. As a boulevardier I would stop and listen to the shrill oriental music played on a kind of bagpipe by a man in bloomers. The music attracted people to a bevy of veiled ladies standing on a high platform while another man told us how they had come from far-off Turkey and Arabia to offer entertainment never before seen in McKeesport. Every now and then they gave brief, confirming jerks when the man said that for fifteen cents one could watch "these lovely ladies dance; not with their feet, not with their hands, but with every little muscle of their quivering bodies." As the performance was always about to begin immediately and was for adults only, I would move on to less perplexing diversions.

Occasionally McKeesport harbored unusual attractions. One day a wonderful stuffed whale in a covered barge was moored next to the Fifth Avenue bridge. From the free lectures delivered by the whale's spokesman I learned that it had been viewed by the crowned heads of Europe and acclaimed by the press and pulpit everywhere as of invaluable educational importance. The day the whale arrived an advertisement in the *Daily News* announced that a full set of furniture would be given by Bowman's Store to the first couple to be married in its mouth. Having a dime, I attended the event and was impressed less by the ceremony than by some information on whales imparted by the lecturer to the paying guests. He said that despite the size of the creature's mouth, roomy enough, as all could see, for a wedding party, nothing larger than an orange could pass through the opening of its throat. This, we were told, was why Jonah had been able to travel in comfort. For several days the whale's mouth was a popular nuptial chapel, but subsequent brides and grooms received only sets of china for their homes.

Throughout the year McKeesport was a favorite haunt of a breed of visitors who never stayed very long but always provided diversion. I didn't know then that they called themselves low pitchmen and high pitchmen. The low pitchmen worked alone. In the evening they would set up collapsible stands in the recessed entrances of stores and office buildings closed for the day. The items in their stock-in-trade were beyond my means, but there were always grown-up customers for such bargains as artistically engraved twenty-four jeweled gold hunting-case watches guaranteed to last a lifetime and beautiful diamond, ruby, and emerald rings and stickpins, unquestionably the finest of gifts for a family man's loved ones.

Other strangers offered everything from new kinds of vegetable cutters at unbelievably low introductory prices to books revealing the secret spells of voodoo priests in India. One evening I saw Mr. Wynn, a policeman friend of mine, arrest a sidewalk merchant before he could escape with his cakes of health soap recognized by doctors everywhere as the world's greatest remover of dandruff, warts, and all other forms of skin blemish. I felt very sorry about the arrest because earlier in the day I had seen the poor man suffer another misfortune. My father had ordered him out of the Hotel White because of the smells that had wafted from the bedroom he was using as a soap factory.

In those days the foreigners who worked in the tube mills and tin-plate factory would buy anything. They almost broke the front window of Mr. Wylie's funeral parlor to enjoy the world of good promised by a man selling medicated peanuts.

In 1902 people were reading in the newspapers that Dutch settlers in South Africa were fighting for independence against the British. The names of Oom Paul Kruger and General Christiaan De Wet were familiar to everyone. Hundreds of Irish mill workers turned out in McKeesport to greet a spokesman for the South Africans. His broad-brimmed black hat, dark suit, knee-length boots, and chin whiskers identified him as one of the gallant Dutchmen whose pictures we had seen. He collected a lot of Irish money for the widows and orphans of the brave Boer soldiers being murdered in the Transvaal by a heartless tyrant called Queen Victoria. I read later that the police in Uniontown had put the false Dutchman in jail.

I was as sorry as anyone for the poor Boers, but that

didn't keep me from enjoying a riddle printed in a current issue of *Drummers' Yarns*, my favorite of all the magazines I constantly browsed through on the depot newsstand:

SMITH: "Why does Oom Paul Kruger wear rubber boots?"

JONESY: "To keep De Wet from defeat."

The high pitchmen were moguls among patent-medicine quacks and ballyhooed their operations. Having rented the vacant lot at Sinclair and Ringgold, they announced their advent in newspaper ads. Watching the arrival of their big wagons was as important to small boys as the appearance of a circus. It was absorbing to see a big van become an elevated stage on which the owner of the outfit would sell his cure-alls. He would make sales talks between the acts of his free vaudeville show just as today's glib talker on TV plugs his tonic between variety turns. The TV smoothies are restrained by law from overpraising their medicines, but the old-timers were unhampered. I doubt that any of them had valid medical degrees, but I can't remember one who did not call himself a doctor. Most were tall, handsome, and portly, and all radiated the perfect health derived from what they sold. Elegant, double-breasted frock coats clearly proved they were men of distinction. One doctor's faun-colored Prince Albert was not unlike that of W.C. Fields's in *Poppy*. Fields said his was made of unborn elephant hide. The doctor's was more elegant. In place of the conventional double row of buttons he used twenty-dollar gold pieces. His promises of costly prizes for winners in a baby contest attracted scores of entrants, eligible to compete after their mothers purchased some of the doctor's world-renowned remedy for female complaint. The big prizes he conferred were like those I had seen lucky players win at carnival wheels-of-fortune, but no baby ever went away trophyless. One night the doctor regretfully told the mother of a belated arrival that the contest was over. The lady tearfully explained that she had come by streetcar all the way from Monongahela City. You could see the doctor felt pretty bad about her plight.

"May I see the baby?"

It was held up for his inspection.

"Madam, that is a very beautiful infant, and I'm going for once to break a rule!"

He turned to an assistant. "Give me the finest prize we have!"

The man had to tell him that all the prizes had been given out. The doctor was chagrined but only for a moment. Then without hesitance he cut one of the gold pieces off his coat.

"With my compliments, Madam," he said. There was loud applause for his warmhearted generosity. Jimmy Wynn, the son of my policeman friend, had hung around the lot all day. I thought he must be mistaken when he said that the lady who got the gold piece was married to the man who said the prizes were all gone.

The faun-coated philanthropist was a pillar of probity compared to others. Their profits did not come entirely from pills and tonics. Before starting an entertainment program, one of them would caution his listeners to make sure their money was safe. He did this, he said, because many old friends were in the audience and while it was unlikely that such a fine group of citizens would include a pickpocket, he had been told that one had recently been arrested in nearby Charleroi. Toward the end of the entertainment the doctor confessed his interest in McKeesport politics. He asked the Republicans and Democrats present to raise their hands in turn. As he counted them slowly, his sleight-of-hand men, who earlier had spotted many pockets being patted, went to work. If one of them was caught, the doctor's earlier words of warning established his own innocence and the pickpocket, more often than not, talked his way to liberty.

Not all high pitchmen were such brazen crooks, but all found old clients in every audience eager to testify that the doctor's medicines had completely freed them of lung trouble, toothache, kidney disease, boils, or approaching baldness.

The benevolent creator of Dr. Walker's Bulgarian Heart Balm opened up shop one night blazing with indignation. He was less concerned with selling his infallible remedy than in exposing an impostor who was skulking about Pennsylvania using his name.

"He is aware," thundered the doctor, "that I always present valuable souvenirs to my friends when they purchase the genuine Bulgarian Balm created in my laboratories and sold only by me. This is how the so-called 'Dr. Walker' works. How many of you got one of his 'solid gold fountain pens' when you paid two dollars for the stuff he was selling?"

A scattering of men held up their hands.

"You gentlemen may not know it, but you were swindled!"

The men dropped their jaws in astonishment.

"Do you happen to have those pens with you?" the doctor asked.

By an odd coincidence they all did.

"Now take a close look at them. Turn up the lights, please, so these good people can see how they were robbed. If you will look closely you will notice that the letter 'g' in 'gold' is actually the letter 'c.' Oh, the fake Dr. Walker is clever, I grant you. By selling you a solid 'cold' pen, he thinks he can keep out of prison, but he won't stay out long if I ever catch up with him!"

Bystanders crowded about the cheated men. When everyone had confirmed the deception, the exposer of professional malpractice revealed his own immaculate ethics.

"Friends," he confessed gravely, "I could not afford to offer you a really fine medicine *and* a real gold fountain pen for two dollars. Neither could any other honest man. Not for five dollars, ten dollars, or twenty dollars. That is if the pen was made of the kind of gold recognized by the United States Assay Office. I know many of you are ready to testify that even a hundred dollars could not begin to pay for the blessings you get from the only genuine Bulgarian Heart Balm. My patients are always asking me: 'Doctor, why on earth do you charge only one dollar a bottle for your priceless medicine?' Friends, the answer is simple. So many great hospitals, medical clinics, and private physicians use and praise my product that the very small profit I make per bottle allows me to live a decent, upright life, ready to look any man in the eye without fear or favor. And that is why tonight I'm continuing to sell the only genuine original Bulgarian Heart Balm at the ridiculously low price of one dollar and present with every bottle a small but valuable gift. It is a fountain pen. It is not stamped either 'solid gold' or 'solid cold.' But anyone with two eyes will see engraved on each and every barrel the words 'Genuine Sterling Silver.' "

You had to move fast to get out of the stampede of customers.

By 1902 half a dozen of McKeesport's vacant stores had been converted into motion picture theaters. They were called nickelodeons, a name that movie historians acknowledge was invented in McKeesport. For five cents you could witness the eruption of Mount Pelée on a film six hundred feet long. You could also see people moving about at the Paris Exposition. Some said watching the pictures would cause blindness, but the nickelodeons survived all criticisms. One 1902 advertisement read: "There will be nothing shown but new up-to-date pictures of things you would have to travel thousands of miles to witness in person."

There were other all-year-round entertainments. My father's friend John Harris operated a vaudeville theater with new acts every week. I was his constant uninvited guest. And Frank Hunter, the manager of White's Opera House and another of my father's friends, eventually reconciled himself to my steady patronage. The visiting stars who performed there on one-night stands always stayed at our hotel. It was exciting to watch Chauncey Olcott eating dinner like anyone else and know that a little later he would thrill McKeesporters, as he had the rest of the nation, singing his latest hit, "My Wild Irish Rose." I first heard "Hearts and Flowers" when the body of a lady, put into a deep sleep by the hypnotic hands and eyes of Kellar the Great, slowly ascended in an incredible feat called "The Levitation of the Princess Karnak." Kellar was America's foremost magician. Passing through the hotel lobby he looked like an ordinary mortal, but whenever I saw the posters and window cards depicting his wonderfully bald head inclined toward the Imp from Hell that was whispering in his ear, I knew he was a wizard and that an evening of eerie excitement was coming. Lew Dockstader's Minstrels made many visits to White's Opera House. Everyone turned out when his company of fifty invariably paraded down Fifth Avenue in full makeup, with a band and banners. Mr. Dockstader always consulted my father on local happenings that might be worked into jokes for his McKeesport engagement.

Despite parental efforts to protect guests from my acquaintance, my favorite hero of the stage became a dear friend. His name was Chester de Vaughn, and life was radiant when his traveling stock company made one of their week-long stays in McKeesport.

On pleasant days the patrons of the Hotel White could tilt back the chairs on the sidewalk in front of the lobby windows and enjoy the sunshine. I often occupied the one next to Chester's, and despite his being a man thirty years of age, he treated me as an equal. We called each other by our first names, and he would tell me where his troupe had last performed, where they were going next, and what plays he would appear in next season. His easy companionship more than compensated for my unfriendly treatment by baseball players from other towns in the Tri-State League when they came for games in McKeesport. The Youngstown team contained the most surly ruffians. The first time they arrived my admiration for athletes prompted me to offer friendly greetings. They were rejected churlishly. Whenever I said hello they would say, "Don't bother me, kid!" They chewed tobacco and used cuss words. Their bad manners made Chester seem godlike.

In those days traveling repertory companies could carry a lot of scenery, because railway fares were low and with the purchase of a small block of tickets a baggage car was provided free. The Chester de Vaughn Stock Company always carried sets for several plays. Chester's scale of prices was ten, twenty, and thirty cents and his audiences always got their money's worth. In the intermission before each last act the main curtain would rise, disclosing another, covered with panels of advertisements on which you could read about Mr. Gusky's gents' furnishings, Mr. Yester's fine jewelry, Spear & Co.'s "Nuf Sed" furniture and the tip-top oyster stews the City Lunch had waiting for those who dropped in after the show. The second curtain would ripple behind him as Chester made his way from the wings in a handsome quilted dressing gown, an elegant scarf tucked into his collar. Lifting his arm like a Roman emperor, he would halt the applause. His speeches went pretty much like this: "Ladies and Gentlemen, tomorrow afternoon, for the first time in my current McKeesport season, theatergoers will be offered that powerful drama of crime and repentance *Jim, the Penman.* Tomorrow night, by popular demand, you will see that classic battle twixt good and evil, *Dr. Jekyll and Mr. Hyde,* in which I will again re-create the dual title roles. Friday night the Chester de Vaughn players will bring you a new serio-comic drama of Anglo–Indian life from my own pen entitled *The Scarlet Z*, replete with gripping suspense and comical episodes. Saturday our concluding matinee audience will again enjoy the thrills and chills of the ever popular favorite *The Cherry Pickers*. And, to conclude our McKeesport season in gales of laughter, on Saturday evening you will see that hilarious farce of farces *Too Much Johnson*. And now, before the curtain rises on the fourth and last act of tonight's performance of *The Ten Ton Door*, may I on behalf of my company and myself bid you, one and all, a very kind good night?"

I was never able to get enough of *The Ten Ton Door*. It too, was a serio-comic drama from Chester's pen. It dealt with the dangers faced by a brave British officer held prisoner in a desert fortress by a band of murderous Arabs. The scene of the third act was a courtyard of the fortress, and in an upstage wall was the enormous portal that gave the play its title. Aware that outnumbering British troops would soon recapture the stronghold, the Arabs had lashed Chester to the door and removed the bolts of its hinges. The snarling Arab chief pointed out that when the first British cannonball struck the door, it would topple inward and crush Chester to death. With blood-curdling cries, the fiends abandoned the fortress. In the distance one heard the bugles of the approaching British. Spread-eagled and hopeless, Chester summed up the situation with a line I have never forgotten: "Chained to the door of death!"

At that moment, who should appear but Sergeant Clancy, a little Irishman who all evening had kept us in hysterics with his laughable sayings. We thought he had been killed like all the rest of Chester's companions. The little Irishman now showed he had more in him than monkeyshines. He darted to Chester and quickly unloosed his bonds. Chester managed to step aside a moment before the door was knocked off its balance by a British cannonball. As the door crashed it raised a cloud of dust the theater stage had been accumulating for years.

I never knew exactly how much the ten-ton door weighed, but it was heavy enough to be very impressive as it fell. One night something went wrong. The door came down with Chester under it. The little Irishman rushed onstage in a panic. The curtain hurriedly descended, and the stunned audience sat breathless, prepared for an announcement of Chester's death. After only a slightly longer wait than usual, Chester himself appeared in the familiar dressing gown and scarf with only a degree less of his customary aplomb. There was a roar of applause. Chester stopped it by raising his right hand as usual. His left held a partially reddened handkerchief to his nose. The audience cheered when he assured us his nose was not broken. Then, heroically dismissing his miraculous escape, he began his routine speech.

"Ladies and Gentlemen, tomorrow afternoon for the first time in our current McKeesport season, the Chester de Vaughn players will bring to you that thrilling drama, the masterpiece of the war between the states, *The Drummer Boy of Shiloh*. Tomorrow night . . ."

It was an early spring day when Chester and I had our last friendly chat. We were sitting side by side, our chairs tipped back as usual. Chester had just told me his company would soon be disbanding for the summer. I was saddened.

"Then I won't see you again for a long time, Chester."

"No, Marcus, I'll probably be in McKeesport lots of time this summer."

My depression vanished. "You will? Why?"

"I guess I never told you that in the summer I play professional baseball. This year I'll be with the Tri-State League. I've signed up as a catcher on the Youngstown team."

Something more crushing than a ten-ton door fell on me.

3

Trinity Hall

IN JUNE, 1902, my father suddenly died of pneumonia. The following September the problem of running a hotel and rearing an eleven-year-old boy simultaneously was eased a bit for my mother when I was enrolled at Trinity Hall, a boarding school in Washington, Pennsylvania. It had been founded under the sponsorship of General Grant in the late seventies as both an English form school and a military academy.

When I entered the first form the school's headmaster and commandant was the general's nephew, Ulysses Grant Smith. Another Grant relative was the rector. The rector had a habit of spoiling everyone's breakfast. All six forms ate simultaneously in a big dining hall. The Rector sat with the principal members of the faculty at one end of the room, facing the tables of the students. The appearance of hot oatmeal or pancakes on cold mornings was a signal the rector always seemed to be waiting for. A loud tapping of his spoon against a water glass arrested the first mouthfuls in midair. Dutifully, all present rose to their feet. The rector beamed benignly, carefully opened a book, and slowly sought and eventually found an elusive page. His audience wondered when icicles would form on their food.

"Boys," he would announce, "let us make our morn-

ing brighter by a few words of Jeremy Taylor." I can still
hear him droning the verses that began:

> Now when the daylight fills the sky
> We lift our hearts to God on high . . .

My thoughts remained below.

The rector was also monotonously unattractive at
morning prayers in the school chapel, but the winners of
the daily struggle to march into devotions beside George
Montgomery, a fourth-former, could always anticipate relief. The lack of oxygen in the chapel often caused George
to faint, but before he could keel over, at least eight willing hands were ready to stay his fall and bear him outside.
The fresh air in the hall immediately revived him, but until
the Rector's final "Amen," the first-aid corps stood by in
case of a recurrence.

Until the school ended its existence in 1907, my
closest friend was Robert Carter. He was called Nick of
course. We were both fifteen and in the fifth form when
we got a new classmate. His name was George Dougherty.
He arrrived at a moment when heavy penalties were being
imposed on any boys caught smoking cigarettes. The few
who experimented with corn silk rolled in toilet paper
found the substitutes unsatisfactory. Suddenly there was a
widespread interest in loose-leaf chewing tobacco, which
could be obtained in the same out-of-bounds shops that
had sold us cigarettes. On his first day at Trinity, Dougherty impressed many of us by his ability to put the entire contents of a bulky package of Polar Bear chewing
tobacco in his mouth. Until then the record had been
held by a thirteen-year-old fourth-former who had done
the same thing with a package of Mail Pouch, which came

in a smaller container. The respect Dougherty gained by his oral capacity was enhanced when he told us he had been expelled from several prep schools for a variety of breaches of discipline. We learned with awe that he had been dismissed even from Culver Military Academy. In those days Culver was famous among school boys for its strict discipline, and being dismissed from there was to us something like being expelled from Alcatraz. Dougherty's prestige waned however when he told us how he had come to Trinity.

A week previous another boarding school had sent him home to Wheeling, West Virginia. While his parents were reconciling themselves to his latest homecoming, Wheeling was inundated by one of the Allegheny River's severe spring floods. The Doughertys became isolated on the upper floor of their dwelling. In a thoughtless moment George's mother allowed him to leave in a skiff, which the household depended on in such emergencies. His instructions were to fetch food, but he became so interested in rescue work elsewhere in the city that he did not return until the flood had receded three days later. When train service was resumed George was placed on one, bound for Trinity Hall. From then on our new classmate was nicknamed Dip, short for Dippy, which was Trinityhallese for crazy.

One day Nick Carter and I wrote our names and address on the triangular coupon we had cut from an advertisement in a magazine, pooled our resources, and sent ten cents for a book of instruction on hypnotism. The book failed to arrive, but that did not discourage our interest. In the town library we learned something about hypnotists' sleep-producing methods. We learned that if a patient watched a spinning multifaceted glass ball while a blue light shone in his eyes, the results were almost immediately effective. Dip offered himself for scientific experiment. Fifth- and sixth-form students had their own rooms, and in the comparative privacy of Nick's, Dip stretched himself out on the bed and invited us to proceed. While Nick made a flashlight shine through the bottom of a Bromo-Seltzer bottle, Dip was instructed to keep his eyes on a Ping-Pong ball a few inches above his nose. The ball was attached to a string, which I rolled between my hands, and gave off flecks of light from bits of broken mirror we had glued to its surface. Part of our everyday vocabulary at Trinity was Archimedes' celebrated exclamation. When we saw Dip slip into insensibility, our "eureka's" were louder than any ever heard in Greece. We felt a witness to our success was needed, so we summoned Doc Thompson, another fifth-former, to confirm our triumph. Doc's father owned a pharmacy in Irwin, Pennsylvania. His closet was filled with items from the drugstore's shelves. (It was from Doc I learned that if you stick your finger into a glass of water the surface of which is coated with lycopodium, your finger will be completely dry when you take it out. Knowing things like that has added greatly to my status as a scientist.)

Any doubt Doc might have had of our ability was dispelled when Dip showed no reaction to a pin stuck in his leg. A few passages of hands above his face and murmured repetitions of "Wake up, Dip" resulted in a fluttering of eyes. A moment later Dip sat up and said he remembered nothing that had happened during his trance. It was agreed that our strange new power should have public recognition. The entire school was invited to attend a

great scientific experiment that night. In the interval between dinner and evening study period, all copies of *The
Illustrated London News, Le Monde Illustre, Punch, Sim-
plicissimus, Die Fliegende Blätter, The Scientific American*
and *Youth's Companion* were removed from the table in
the reading room. Masters and prefects watched apprehen-
sively as Dip stretched himself out on the table, unconcerned by the collection of pins, needles, surgical skewers,
and other implements Doc Thompson had assembled in his
self-appointed role of associate. There were a good many
faculty frowns as the mesmeric talents of professors Carter
and Connelly were demonstrated. Dip's eyes closed immediately, and he was shown to be immune to our assistant's
needles and pins. Larger instruments were then produced,
but faculty members, rousing themselves from their own
near-hypnotic states, forbade their employment. Nick and
I then deftly brought Dip back to consciousness. Again he
asked what had happened while he was asleep. Several
masters honored us by being baffled. Yet, despite our success, Nick and I were told that no more demonstrations
would be allowed. It was a blow to our pride and an
affront to our skill. We privately raged against the arbitrary blocking of studies preparatory to careers for which
we were obviously qualified. We considered leaving
school and making our fortunes in vaudeville. We so
informed our parents. Only immediate and emphatic parental forbiddance delayed us from notifying B. F. Keith of
our availability.

Spring examinations were approaching, and our gall-
ing frustration was assuaged a bit by Doc Thompson's
amazing discovery of a solution to a thorny academic
problem. The fifth form felt sure that the civics test would

demand a listing of the order of succession of the Cabinet to the Presidency of the United States. It was clearly stated in a textbook as follows: Secretary of State, Secretary of the Treasury, Secretary of War, the Attorney General, the Postmaster General, Secretary of the Navy, Secretary of the Interior, Secretary of Agriculture, and the Secretary of Commerce and Labor. Unhappily the book would not be available during the test. Today we live in a world of acronyms. My first was the one Doc Thompson invented. On the day of the examination it was chalked all over the classroom blackboards, floor, and ceiling. Mr. Sears, the Civics master, was noticeably baffled by the omnipresence of the word: STWAPNIAC. At least one question in the exam was answered correctly.

A week or two later the plans of Carter and Connelly for a theatrical career were abruptly abandoned. One morning Dip stopped us on our way to class. Sitting in the recess of a hall window, he had watched us approach, grinning.

"What's on your mind?" asked Nick.

"Oh, nothing," drawled Dip. "I was just thinking what dopes you two are." He laughed idiotically. "Judas Priest, did I make monkeys out of you!"

With asinine snorts Dip told us that during our experiments he had only pretended to be hypnotized. When he showed us an old scar on his arm which had resulted from a competition somewhere with another boy in the application of hot nails, we believed him.

When I was twelve, and in the second form, most classroom hours were periods of forced labor. Encouragement to enjoy what we were learning was seldom offered. We were ignorant of why we had to learn this or that, like animals responding to Clyde Beatty's whip. We were aware that good marks were desirable, but little was done to quicken our interest and make our education a true "drawing forth." Because inculcation was the common practice of our trainers, the bell at the end of a class meant a momentary removal of fetters. My appetite for reading helped me get through the *New Gradatim* and *Gestae Romanorum* with a minimum of agony, but the dullness of Caesar's *Commentaries* destroyed any waking interest in Latin. About all I remember of them today is that during his invasions, Caesar encountered many individuals whose names either began with or contained the letter *v*.

The discovery that education need not always cause anguish came to me unexpectedly. The boys in the lower forms slept in alcoves in a dormitory. Individual privacy was provided by a linen curtain in each cubicle, but because the curtains were transluscent, great care had to be taken to shade the forbidden flashlight by which one read clandestinely or the flame of the sterno lamp over which one heated small cans of beans when famine struck in the night. It was about ten. The dormitory was in darkness. I had heated some beans to enjoy while indulging in a bit of illicit reading. A sound outside my alcove suggested the approach of a prowling prefect or master. I turned out my concealed light and listened. Again the dormitory was silent, but I was cautious. In the dark I spooned a few beans from the tin, brooding over the police-state life led by the lower-formers. "Why," I mused, "should this wonderful book be readable only at the risk of corporal punishment?

Why should any fair-minded person object to my enjoying it? There were books we had to read in third-form English that—"

A lightning flash of recollection demolished my resentment. I was not obliged to read this book surreptitiously. It was one we were presently studying in class. Its title was *David Copperfield*.

When the third form was studying *The Idylls of the King* I was told to memorize a passage from "The Passing of Arthur" for the customary Friday declamation hour. I did so easily. (Even today I can rattle off a good deal of what happened after the noise of battle had rolled all day among the mountains by the winter sea, leaving King Arthur a broken chancel with a broken cross.) When I rose to recite I had the passage down letter-perfect and I was self-confident. I finished and expected hearty approval from my teacher, possibly flattering compliments. Instead he looked at me inquisitively and asked me to repeat the concluding lines. I graciously responded with an encore:

"But now delay not: take Excalibur,
"And fling him far into the middle mere:
"Watch what thou seest, and lightly bring me word."
To him replied the bold Sir Bedivere:

Again applause was withheld.

"Yes, I thought that was what I heard, Connelly. May I ask if you are trying to be facetious?"

The question was bewildering. I said I wasn't.

"Do you think what you have recited makes sense?"

With quiet dignity I said I thought it did.

"Well, instead of stopping at a colon in the middle of a statement, suppose you tell us Bedivere's reply to King Arthur's command."

I said I didn't know.

"Why don't you know?"

"Because you told me to learn at least thirty-five lines. I learned two more."

The master stared. Silently I watched him open a copy of *The Idylls*. He examined the text.

"Connelly," he said contritely, "I had judged you to be a complete idiot. I have done you an injustice. I have discovered you can count."

Sometimes old storage bins in a writer's mind provide material for fictitious use, and in the early 1930s, when I was adapting Kipling's *Captains Courageous* for a motion picture, I felt it necessary to establish the character of Harvey, the young hero, before he boarded the ocean liner from which he was to fall into the sea. If you should ever see it on television's Late Late Show you will find another schoolboy unable to report what Sir Bedivere replied. And to this day neither can I.

One more incident at Trinity may merit recounting. When I was in the fifth form, Finis Montgomery, an uncle of George, the fainter, had become our headmaster. He had come from Washington and Jefferson, where his outstanding record at football had caused Walter Camp, then the country's foremost sports authority, to name him an all-American quarterback. At Trinity Hall I played right guard on our first team, and my one hundred and fifty-six pounds made me useful in flying-wedge plays, which were then legal. On the day of our annual game with Shadyside Academy in Pittsburgh, our fullback came down with the mumps. We had no substitute with even a tenth of his ability until our new headmaster, swearing us to silence, stepped into the breach. He was unrecognizable under the big rubber noseguard and other headgear worn by all players, and he did not weigh much more than our sick fullback. The presence of an illustrious all-American was an inspiration to our team. He must have overawed us. I remember that Shadyside beat us pretty badly.

4

The Road to New York

I HAD EXPECTED to go to Harvard, but a financial panic in 1908 ended all hope of my going to any college. Through bankruptcy my mother lost the new Hotel White which she had built the previous year. We were obliged to move to Pittsburgh and live with my father's sister and brother-in-law until my mother opened a small dress shop in the Liberty Arcade and I got a job on a newspaper.

At first, the job consisted of walking several miles a day to collect money owed for classified ads in the Pittsburgh *Press*. I forget what I was paid. It couldn't have been much, because my daily collections seldom amounted to more than five or six dollars. Somehow I became acquainted with Albert Barr, the paper's publisher. I told him I wanted to be a writer. The *Press* was in receivership, and perhaps because he felt that the paper had nothing to lose, Mr. Barr allowed me to concoct the most wretched attempt at humorous writing a newspaper ever inflicted on its readers. Finley Peter Dunne's *Mr. Dooley* was then at the peak of popularity and he was the inspiration for my intendedly droll observations of an Irish policeman. I even had the gall to make him speak in a brogue that must have curdled the blood of its readers.

Eventually Max Swain of the Pittsburgh Associated Press office, a rewrite man, got me a job as a cub reporter for the AP. After a few months I was editing the "pony

4 0

wire," which meant rewriting and cutting news items to fill the orders of small-town papers that could not afford the full AP service.

A year or so later I had become competent enough to be taken on as a legman by the *Gazette Times*, Pittsburgh's biggest paper. My mother and I were able to move to a small flat in the Oakland section of Pittsburgh near the Carnegie Institute and Forbes Field, the home of the Pittsburgh Pirates. My mother's shop made little profit, but I was able to support us handsomely. Not only was I earning twenty-two dollars a week as a reporter, but a Sunday humorous column called "Jots and Tittles" brought in a cool six dollars more. "Jots and Tittles" was inspired by the brilliant miscellany in Bert Leston Taylor's daily "Line O' Type" column in the Chicago *Tribune* and his protégé Franklin Pierce Adams' "Conning Tower" in the New York *Post*. My new column was considerably better than my imitation of Mr. Dooley, being mostly made up, as were my mentors', of items culled from other papers and spiced by editorial comment. Some of my quips were mildly funny; I remember one in particular. I had clipped from *Pennsylvania Grit* a bona-fide news item reporting a family reunion. The family had the odd surname of Foor. The Foors' given names seemed noteworthy too; they included Ona, Ina, Eva, Ida, Tina, and several other bisyllables. To this day I could murder the higher editorial authority who decided that my caption for the item, "All Present or Accounted Foor," contained a superfluous o.

The Voice in the Rice and other stories then being written for *The Saturday Evening Post* by Gouverneur Morris entranced me. His *Putting on the Screws*, the bittersweet story of a rich and eccentric old actress who tested the affection of distant relatives by pretending to be deaf and broke, struck me as wonderfully promising dramatic material. I was seventeen then and charged with self-confidence, so I boldly wrote to Mr. Morris, suggesting that he let me adapt it for the stage. He undoubtedly recognized the callowness reflected in my letter, yet his courteous response was that of one professional craftsman writing to another. He wrote that he was delighted to learn that I had liked *Putting on the Screws* but that unfortunately its dramatic rights had already gone to someone else. I never met Mr. Morris, but when I became a little drier behind the ears, I realized what he did for my ego in his friendly reply.

As a reporter, I met Oliver Nicola, a wealthy man-about-town and influential member of the Pittsburgh Athletic Association. Through him, I acquired a free membership in the P.A.A. In exchange, the club had my services as the director–stage manager of monthly entertainments in the clubhouse theater. I wrote several skits for the shows. Charles M. Bregg, the *Gazette Times's* drama critic, a giant of letters in my eyes, was kind to a green and cocky nineteen-year-old playwright by letting me be his second-string critic when the Nixon and the Alvin, Pittsburgh's two legitimate theaters, had simultaneous openings. I was able to feast on the performances of such artists as Minnie Maddern Fiske, E. H. Sothern and his wife, Julia Marlowe, Madge Kennedy, Marie Doro, Lulu Glaser, and an endless parade of first-class vaudeville acts at the Davis. Pittsburgh also had two flourishing stock companies. I often reported on their weekly changes of bill. The Pittsburgh Press Club had offices on the tenth floor of a building connected by a back alleyway to the stage entrance of the Belasco Theatre, which housed the Harry Davis Stock Company. Thurston Hall, their leading man, who later became well known in Hollywood, was a devoted poker player. Every night during the performance he proved himself also an athlete. He would exit from a scene and dash up to the Press Club. After playing a few hands he would say "Deal me out" and rush back to the theater. He never missed an entrance cue.

The *Gazette Times* was a morning paper. Its city-room staff arrived at 1:30 P.M. When the last regular edition went to press, shortly after midnight, the city editor would call out "Thirty!" the traditional signal used by telegraph operators to indicate the workday's end. Sometimes I would be assigned to the "lobster" shift, the rotating skeleton staff on duty until three o'clock for bulletins that might require extra editions. Whether I was on late duty or not, I often stayed at my typewriter to work on skits for the P.A.A.

I was twenty-two when a little theater group accepted a one-act play of mine for production. It was a golden moment when I saw cards in store windows that read:

TWO NEW PLAYS BY PITTSBURGH PLAYWRIGHTS

There was my name beside that of Mary Roberts Rinehart! Her first novel, *The Circular Staircase*, had already made her nationally known. Mrs. Rinehart's first play, also a one-act piece, and mine were acted together on two evenings. I cannot remember anything about mine except that its title was *$2.50* and that it was meant to be a comedy dealing with a poor young man's desperate need for a little cash. I did not meet Mrs. Rinehart until a decade later, when we were both living in New York and became good friends. I confessed to her my regret that I couldn't remember the name of her play. She laughed. "I remember *yours*. The club's regular patrons didn't read the ads very carefully and thought your two dollars and a half an outrageously high admission price. We didn't do much business!"

In 1914 Mr. Nicola and several other wealthy P.A.A. members felt that the club had so many fine amateur actors that their talents merited wider exhibition than the monthly clubhouse shows. Alfred Ward Birdsall, also a member, wrote the libretto of a light opera, and Zoel Parenteau, a Pittsburgh composer, was commissioned to write the music. I was trusted with writing the lyrics of the songs. R. H. Burnside, who had directed most of Charles Dillingham's biggest successes, was brought on from New York to stage the production. It was called *The Lady of Luzon* and ran for a week at the Alvin Theater. Oddly enough it was an immense success. Parenteau's music and Burnside's direction had real merit. My lyrics were singable, but that's the most I can say for them.

Billy Bryant, on whose floating theater Edna Ferber did much of her research for *Show Boat*, was once asked why a production of *Hamlet* which he admitted was appallingly bad had enjoyed great success up and down the river for years. "The reason is simple," said Bryant. "In the towns we play, people will go anywhere there are chairs." *The Lady of Luzon*'s patrons must have been of an even more avid breed. They had an unnatural appetite for standing room.

Burnside was probably more astonished by the play's

drawing power than anyone else. When he went back to
New York to prepare the following season's spectacle at
the New York Hippodrome, he took with him a song Zoel
and I had written at his suggestion. It was to be my first
writing for the theaters of New York. Called "My Land!
My Flag!" it was sung a few months later on the gigantic
Hippodrome staged by two hundred Boy and Girl Scouts.
They stood on tiers like a football cheering section, and as
they sang, the chorus turned into a living star-spangled
banner.

One of the sponsors of *The Lady of Luzon* was a
stagestruck steel magnate named Joseph Riter. In New
York he had presented two hits—*Erstwhile Susan*, with
Mrs. Fiske, and Marian de Forrest's dramatization of *Little
Women*. Recklessly, Riter next commissioned Zoel and me
to write a comic opera, which he promised to produce.
We decided to call it *The Amber Empress*. I had found a
book dealing with the legends of historical villas between
Padua and Venice and chose the story of the young
architect who had to design the Villa Frigimelica for the
girl he loved as a wedding gift from the ageing doge she
was forced to marry. It was a good story and stirred Zoel to
write a score of fresh and appealing charm. By that time, I
was a little more proficient at verse writing, and I remember the words I wrote for a barcarole. It was ingenious
rather than meritorious, consisting entirely of leonine
rhymes, every iambic accent in one line rhyming with its
equivalent in the next. Here are two of the couplets:

> Farewell, poor moon so cold and lorn
> Thy knell the boon of golden morn
> The sun must reign up there alone
> With none he'll deign to share his throne.

Riter opened offices in New York for his productions and engaged a man who had been with Henry Savage, the producer of *The Chocolate Soldier* and other hits, as his general manager. There's probably a Freudian significance in my not being able to recall his name. He read *The Amber Empress* and recommended that the book and lyrics be rewritten entirely by more experienced hands. I don't know of any libretto ever having so many professionals rewrite it. Riter accepted every nominee recommended by his general manager. Dozens of lyric writers in New York had a crack at writing new words for Zoel's music. When the play opened at the Colonial in Boston, the story still had an Italian background. It had been brought up to date and dealt with the adventures of an American motion-picture company in Venice. I was taken along on the try-out as a guest of the management and observer of the production. By this time, all that remained of what I had written were the words of two of the songs and the show's title. In Boston more doctors were brought in. Two weeks later, when *The Amber Empress* opened on Broadway, my title was still used, but now only one song had been part of the original score. Although every trace of my libretto had disappeared, those who had improved it were all foxy enough to remain anonymous. Marcus C. Connelly was the only culprit cited in a set of reviews that were all obituaries. Because the audiences in Boston had consisted largely of the librettist currently engaged in the daily changes or those brought up from New York and waiting their turn, my royalties were meager. When the scenery of *The Amber Empress* quickly moved from the Globe Theater to Cain's theatrical storehouse I didn't have train fare back to Pittsburgh. However, Carl Keffer, who had been a fellow reporter in Pittsburgh, had got a job as an advertising writer in New York, and he let me stay with him while I looked for work. It was hard to find, and the day before I was about to pawn my watch, thieves broke into his flat next to Keen's Chop House on West Thirty-sixth Street. My watch was stolen.

Zoel's talent had not gone unrecognized. Soon he was back in New York, writing the score for another musical piece being prepared by Raymond Hitchcock, one of the drollest of America's great comedians. Henry Blossom, also very successful as the author of several of Victor Herbert's operettas, had been engaged to write the book and lyrics. I don't know whether it was flagging energy or the demands of his social life, but something made Blossom feel the need of a ghost-writer. Zoel recommended me, and soon I was having another opportunity to be heard on Broadway, this time under a more illustrious name.

The most successful song Blossom ever wrote with Herbert was "Kiss Me Again," and its history is unique in American songwriting. *Mlle. Modiste* was on the road in its tryout when Fritzi Scheff, the diminutive star, insisted on a replacement for a number she felt did not give her voice sufficient range. Victor Herbert, one of the few musicians who developed his compositions on a cello, had, like most tunesmiths, a portfolio of unused melodies. He played one for Blossom. As lyric writers have done since the craft began, Blossom jotted down a "dummy" lyric, a series of improvised words and phrases which gave the stresses, rhythm, and rhyme schemes on which the ultimate lyric would be modeled. The new song was wanted for immediate inclusion in the score. Blossom promised to have it ready the following morning. Unfortunately, a seizure of ptomaine poisoning abruptly halted all work on the lyric. At the next night's performance the song was sung with the words Blossom had scribbled as guideposts. They were sung so successfully, Blossom told me, that except for a change of two or three minor words, the world has ever since been singing the "dummy" lyric to "Kiss Me Again!"

I was not allowed to go near rehearsals when the new show—it was called *Follow the Girl*—opened in Philadelphia. The fifty dollars I had been paid for the lyrics of half a dozen songs was about gone. Zoel paid my fare to Philadelphia and smuggled me into his room in Green's Hotel. I ate in obscure restaurants to keep my presence from being discovered. Hitchcock had decided on Philadelphia for the tryout as he would be appearing in a neighboring theater in one of his invariably successful *Hitchy-koo* revues and could oversee the Blossom–Parenteau production. I got daily reports from Zoel on how the show was going. His accounts were not overly encouraging. I spent my time seeing the sights of Philadelphia and writing verses I hoped to sell to magazines one day.

The week before Christmas used to be the worst week in the year for theaters, which partly accounted for the poor business both *Follow the Girl* and *Hitchy-koo* were doing. However, I had almost forgotten that it was Christmas Eve when I was sneaking back into Zoel's hotel room late one night. I passed an open bedroom door and saw three of Hitchcock's *Hitchy-koo* nymphets trimming their Christmas tree. The box-office slump had not dampened their spirits, and they invited me to join them. The gayest and brightest said her name was June Walker. A few years later she was to become one of Broadway's most popular stars, and I had the good luck to write one of her most successful roles, the small, spunky heroine in *The Farmer Takes a Wife*.

When *Follow the Girl* closed on Broadway after a modest run, all I had received from Blossom besides the fifty-dollar fee was the privilege of calling him "Harry," which indicated his acceptance of me as a familiar.

Back in New York I won five dollars from the New York *Sun* in a contest for a five-hundred-word short story, and the broad verse-buying policy of Charles Dana Gibson's humorous weekly, *Life*, brought me enough to keep me alive.

Then, I had a momentary period of prosperity. Probably because I looked threadbare, another former Pittsburgher, now the casting director for a motion-picture studio, got me a job as a scenarist on a movie serial in which Francis X. Bushman and his wife, Beverly Bayne, were to star. William Taylor, the former husband of Laurette Taylor and quite deaf, was the chief scenarist. He already had another assistant, a part-Indian named Jimmy Youngbear. The picture was called *The Great Secret* and was being made in a studio near Tenth Avenue in the West Forties. I never found out what the great secret was and I don't think anyone else working on the picture

knew either. Our daily story conferences consisted mostly
of Mr. Taylor's barking "What, what?" at any suggestions that came from Youngbear and me. The director had
told us that our job was merely to think up predicaments
for the stars to get in and out of, always, of course,
through the ingenuity of the hero. Getting attractive an-
gles of Bushman's head concerned the director as much as
the plot.

"You boys give me the escapes, but don't ever get his
face so dirty I can't get a good profile." Under the supervision of Mr. Taylor, Jimmy and I put Mr. Bushman
through the sewers of New York, a coal mine, and a tong
war in Chinatown, without a smudge on his face. Now
and then the story permitted moments of quiet, poetic
beauty. I remember one so lyrical that Jimmy, its creator,
was so moved as he outlined it to Mr. Taylor and me, that
his voice dropped almost to a whisper:

"And den," said Jimmy, "Bevy taps his face with de
rose, kinda smiles up at him like she was saying 'I ain't an
iceberg.' Den, if you please, she turns on her heel and
walks outa de ballroom. So what does Frank do but turn
away thunderstruck! Den he looks down, and what's at
his feet, but de rose. He picks it up in a kinda trance, because now he knows it's him alone she adores." Here Jimmy's voice dropped to a new low in reverence. "And as he
softly presses the rose to his mouth, we fade—a bewteeful,
slow fade."

Mr. Taylor had been moving up closer to Jimmy, his
hand cupped to his ear. "What? What?" he barked. The
poetic mood was broken.

I was very happy working on *The Great Secret* because I was being paid the unbelievable sum of fifteen dollars a day. When I got my first week's salary, I decided to celebrate it by having a fine dinner in a good restaurant. A very small pearl in an oyster caused me to break a front tooth and forty dollars of my new wealth went to a dentist. However, by the time Mr. Taylor decided he could get along without me I had amassed enough money to send some to my mother and return to Carl Keffer what I had borrowed from him.

Carl was about to get married, so I moved around the corner to 39 West Thirty-seventh Street, where for two dollars a week for lodging I became one of a company of seven artists and writers sharing two rooms. It was quite a heterogeneous collection of strugglers. Our earnings did little more than pay our individual shares of $2 a week for the rooms. The landlady had a handicap unfortunate for the proprietress of a rooming house, a combination of sympathy for and generosity toward her clients. Her name was Roselle Knott, and in her younger days she had been Richard Mansfield's leading lady. Her daughter, Viola, named for Mrs. Knott's favorite Shakespearian heroine, suffered from the same lack of business acumen as her mother. Each would insist that the other make at least an effort to get some money from their roomers, promise to do so, and then duck the obligation.

There was a stretch of sixteen weeks when I was in arrears. I'll never forget when Mrs. Knott cornered me in a hallway and hesitantly observed that I owed her thirty-two dollars. I expected her observation to be followed by instructions to leave, instead of which she looked at me sternly.

"Furthermore," she said, "I don't think you're getting enough to eat!" and walked away before I could thank her for the two dollars she had put in my hand.

In 1934, when *The Green Pastures* troupe of nearly a hundred Negro actors arrived for a performance in Duluth, they discovered that through a flaw in otherwise excellent logistics no housing had been arranged for them. A Methodist minister quickly organized the city's clergy, and within an hour the entire company was comfortably housed. Looking into what might have been a near-tragedy, I discovered that the minister's wife had been of great help in seeing that the troupe had been lodged and fed. Before her marriage she had been Viola Knott.

In the Thirty-seventh Street days, Viola and her mother frequently were unable to supply heat for the house. The winter of 1916 was one of the coldest of the century. I had to wear two pairs of woolen gloves when I tramped over to Pennsylvania Station post office one early March night to mail my mother my weekly letter of baseless enthusiasm over my prospects. The greatest earnings in our group came from the flower and vegetable drawings made by two of my talented roommates. One was John Held, his sheiks and shebas still waiting to be born, and Hal Burroughs, unaware that he would later draw the Metro-Goldwyn-Mayer lion for thousands of posters and other ads.

The larger of the two rooms—the pair was aptly called "Cockroach Glades"—was lighted at night by two gas jets. On very cold nights there was always considerable discussion as to whether we should put a heating contrivance on one of the jets, which would lessen the chattering of teeth but allow only enough light for the creation of a single moss rose or cauliflower. The drawings brought fifty cents each, and despite the drop in income the vote usually went in favor of immediate creature comfort. The lowest ebb of my own fortune was reached one noontime when Johnny, having been rewarded with a dollar instead of fifty cents for an elaborate cluster of strawberries, invited the entire fellowship to a nearby bar for a celebrative round of beer. Beer cost five cents a glass. Having had no breakfast, my host allowed me to toast him with a five cent dill pickle instead.

One afternoon Mrs. Knott burst into our quarters with the news that the daughter of a friend who had been visiting had suddenly been stricken with appendicitis. It was easy to carry Miriam Hopkins down four flights of stairs to an ambulance. She was just thirteen and weighed less than seventy pounds.

In Cockroach Glades we lived on laughter more than any other nourishment. Poverty was a constant depressant but we were all certain of brighter tomorrows. John Held's nimble brain was constantly trying to find ways of making money quickly. The awesomeness of one scheme can best be appreciated with the knowledge that the seven members of the Glades fellowship slept in two beds and two cots. Red Baker, who worked as a night editor for the AP, and Paul Perez, who was an actor, slept during the day, so the five others were not too cramped at night. There was a routine drenching of the legs of beds and cots with roach repellent before we went to sleep. Someone had given John four Airedale puppies, and he complained that their growth was being stunted by the bug spray. We complained that they yipped all night. So John sold the puppies on street corners. With the night-long barking now silenced, the Glades returned to its normal state of quiet misery.

The first World War broke up what had become a fraternity. Most of the group were soon in uniform. I had just landed a job as a reporter on the *Morning Telegraph*. Because I was my mother's sole means of support, I was classified on a deferred list and the war ended before my number came up.

In 1917 and 1918 the *Morning Telegraph* printed so much theatrical news that it was known as the chorus girl's breakfast. Louella Parsons was its motion-picture editor, and Heywood Broun was among the feature writers on its Sunday magazine, of which the celebrated Theodora Bean was the editor. The one and original Bat Masterson was head of the sports department. One night he strolled into the city room from his office on the Fiftieth Street side and broke up a poker game with a casual: "Like to see a bit of shooting, boys? There's some going on down the street."

As we dashed to his office we heard revolver shots. We got to the window in time to see the end of a duel. The obvious loser was sitting on the sidewalk a few feet below us. A man and woman (the man still holding a pistol) stared at the victim from across the street. Before the cops arrived, the pair unhurriedly walked toward Broadway and disappeared down into the subway entrance.

Another important figure on the *Telegraph*, Rennold Wolf, who was coauthor with Channing Pollock of many popular songs, skits for the Ziegfeld Follies, and one or two Broadway shows, had a daily Broadway news column. Every day I had to supply him with breezy chatter I gleaned from several hours' coverage of managers' offices, theater lobbies, and backstage areas.

George S. Kaufman, the drama-section reporter of *The New York Times*, prowled the same neighborhood, and we would see each other every day. George, too, had come from Pittsburgh, and he had had more success there selling shoe findings than I had had with newspaper reporting. We enjoyed each other's company, and because both of us wanted to be playwrights we were constantly tossing ideas about, hoping to find one exciting enough to justify intensive collaboration.

George C. Tyler was one of New York's most important producers. He had made a fortune from *The Man from Home, The Garden of Allah,* and a dozen other hits. One of them, *Alias Jimmy Valentine,* based on O. Henry's story, owed some of its celebrity to Paul Armstrong's dramatization of it within three days in his Hotel Algonquin bedroom.

Mr. Tyler commissioned George Kaufman to adapt Jacques Duval's French farce *Some One in the House.* George did a good job, but a weak cast plus a city-wide epidemic of influenza shortened its life. Tyler reluctantly turned down George's suggestion for an advertising slogan for the faltering play: "Avoid crowds, see *Some One in the House* at the Knickerbocker Theater."

My own big opportunity came when Tyler told me he was thinking of reviving *Erminie,* a famous operetta of the eighties. He liked my ideas for bringing it up to date as a vehicle for those two great comedians DeWolf Hopper and Francis Wilson.

Again I found myself in Boston's Colonial Theater. This time, I heard applause instead of the deathly silence that had attended *The Amber Empress*. Hopper and Wilson gave wonderful buffoon performances. The score, including the widely popular lullaby that one can still hear today, was brilliantly sung. The strikingly original scenery also evidenced Tyler's encouragement of young talents. It was the first Broadway effort of Norman Bel Geddes. Part of the effectiveness was due to the ingenious lighting Norman applied to its basic coloring of several shades of gray. A few weeks later *Erminie* opened at the Park Theater on Columbus Circle and had a fine run.

By now my circle of acquaintances was constantly increasing and included many of the young men and women who wrote humorous verse or prose and woke up most days with the hope that Franklin P. Adams—F.P.A.—had liked and printed their latest contributions in his "Conning Tower" in the *World*. Having your work printed there was a kind of accolade. Usually "Conning Tower" items were signed by pseudonyms or initials. What was important was the individuality of the work rather than the identity of the individual who wrote it. Even before I knew Deems Taylor, there were scores of mornings when breakfast had an extra zest because of something in the "Tower" signed "Smeed." Sometimes it was a triolet or a ballade—"Smeed" was a master of *vers de société*—witty aphorism or a comment on a subject of current interest. One day you would read a gay, iridescent example of verbal bubble-blowing because Smeed had been in the mood for blowing bubbles. On other mornings you would find him being delicately ironic with watercolor brushes or the needles of a silverpoint etcher. When something provoked his contempt, his scorn could come from a machine gun. The only thing not straightforward about *Smeed* was the way he spelled his name.

Once a year the identity of "Conning Tower" contributors would be disclosed at an annual dinner at the Majestic Hotel when the "contribs," as they called themselves, and the Boss, as F.P.A. was affectionately known, would get together for an evening of fun. You could read the pen name of a fellow guest on the card pinned to his or her clothing. The big moment was the presentation by the Boss of a watch to the writer of the item he considered the best printed in the "Tower" during the year. I can't remember how many times Deems Taylor went home with one of the watches, but I can still hear F.P.A. saying "Tonight, I set no precedent, it goes to *Smeed*."

And I can't recall any dinner when everyone there didn't approve of the Boss's choice.

I could now afford to live in something more comfortable than a rooming house, and when Deems suggested that I share his apartment on East Eightieth Street I did. It was over a garage and was bright and comfortable, though its only entrance was by a flight of outside steps. A third member of the household was the current representative of a dynasty of cats. Over the years Deems always kept a cat. Each was called Mrs. Higgins. The only Mrs. Higgins whose conduct I ever heard Deems criticize was one he had many years later when he was living on Fifth Avenue at Sixtieth Street. I had dropped in for cocktails and asked about the well-being of the latest Mrs. Higgins.

"I don't really know what is happening to this one,

but I have suspicions," said Deems. "Let me show you."

Deems was now famous as a composer, and a phonograph company had sent him an album of Cardinal Spellman's sermons. As he put one of its records on the turntable he remarked, "You should know that Mrs. Higgins completely ignores Bach, jive, and everything between them. Now watch her."

The moment the Cardinal's voice was heard, Mrs. Higgins abandoned her windowseat inspection of Central Park, leaped to the phonograph, and, facing it, listened with riveted attention.

Deems whispered, "She hasn't yet learned to kiss rings, but she sneaks out of the house every day to take instruction."

Had a stranger walked into the apartment on Eightieth Street he might have thought half a dozen people worked in our living room, because of Deems's many activities. When Christmas holidays approached, Deems designed wonderfully ribald greeting cards for friends. They were triumphs of Gothic script and elaborate monkish illuminations. Deems could also devise extraordinarily good monograms. He regarded every fresh group of initials as an appetizing challenge. Sometimes they would result in wonderfully fantastic interweavings. Sometimes they were as simple and beautiful as Doric columns.

George Kaufman and his young wife, Beatrice, also lived in the Eighties, but on the West Side. Night after night, after our papers went to press, George and I would walk uptown with each other, discussing ideas that might be dramatic material. One night George said that during the afternoon, Tyler had made a suggestion that seemed worthwhile developing. J. Hartley Manners, who had

written *Peg O' My Heart* and many other plays for his
wife, Laurette Taylor, had, at Laurette's insistence, been
writing increasingly important ingénue parts for a young
English actress named Lynn Fontanne. Although the girl
was under a long-term contract to them, author and star
both agreed with George Tyler that Lynn Fontanne's
talents merited a play of her own.

A nebulous character called Dulcinea with a habita-
tion only in F.P.A.'s imagination frequently popped up in
the "Conning Tower," uttering contemporary clichés as
newly minted wit: "When I want a policeman I can never
find one," "It never rains if I have my umbrella," etc. George
and I felt that a young wife, addicted to bromides, and her
well-meaning but almost disastrous attempts to help her
husband's business career seemed right up Lynn Fontanne's street. When we presented an expansion of the idea
to Tyler and Lynn Fontanne, both agreed with us. All our
free hours were spent on building the outline of the play.
George and I established working methods then that we
followed through all the years we worked together. Having decided that our play should be in a mood of warm
but satiric comedy, we first fumbled about trying to visu-
alize characters and plot progression. As Dulcinea—immediately shortened to Dulcy—was to be a girl of eccentric
impulses, we saw possibilities in her engaging as a butler a
convicted thief, out of jail on probation. She was also the
kind of girl who would invite, among ill-assorted weekend
guests, an egomaniac movie producer, so we invented one
she had met at a dinner party. Quickly the characters,
their development, and the narrative progression were
sketched in great detail. Within a few days we had a completely articulated synopsis of about twenty-five pages.

We then individually chose scenes for which we had predilections, wrote drafts, and then went over them together for improvement. Sometimes each would like the other's writing of a scene enough to let it stand for the final draft, but most passages were the result of considerable rewriting. George's wit sparkled on everything we did. The only areas in our plays which he shied from were love scenes. When we were writing *Merton of the Movies*, our third success, and later *Beggar on Horseback*, George would shiver slightly at my suggestion that he write at least a first draft of sentimental passages. I've often wondered whether he manifested the same aversion with later collaborators.

We completed *Dulcy* in less than a month. I remember beginning the first draft of the third act while I was in Boston watching the tryout of *Erminie*.

Tyler had engaged an excellent cast to support Lynn Fontanne in *Dulcy*. Gregory Kelly, a brilliant juvenile married to Ruth Gordon, was cast as Dulcy's younger, sardonic brother, philosophically reconciled to all of Dulcy's *gaffes* as acts of God. Elliott Nugent was wonderfully amusing as an early form of Madison Avenue advertising man. Wallis Clark played a choleric businessman who, through an entire weekend, found life hell on earth under Dulcy's hospitality. Norma Lee played the tycoon's daughter. (Before the season ended Elliott and Norma were married. In 1966, I attended their forty-fifth wedding anniversary party at The Players Club.)

One of Tyler's most brilliant strokes was in assigning the double chore of directing the play and acting the role of a movie writer to a young actor in the cast, Howard Lindsay.

Booth Tarkington was a close friend of Tyler's. Partly to obtain Tarkington's comments on *Dulcy*, the play opened in Indianapolis, Tarkington's home. His enthusiastic comments were most encouraging and so were the laughter and applause of *Dulcy*'s first audience. After a successful week's run at the Hanna Theater in Indianapolis, we faced a more crucial opening in Chicago.

Chicago was then an important theater city with forty-four theaters healthily competing with one another throughout the year. *Dulcy* was booked into the Cort. On opening night George's exhilaration over the business in Indianapolis had disappeared, replaced by a depression I could not understand. At dinner before the performance, I tried to determine its cause. All I could get from him was a grim statement, "We've been kidding ourselves and we might as well admit it." His discouragement puzzled me, because with the royalties from the Indianapolis performances I would have the most money I had ever made in a week. Moreover, Margalo Gillmore, in my eyes the most enchanting creature on earth, was going to be sitting with me at the performance. Critics who had seen her debut the year before in James Forbes's *The Famous Mrs. Fair* had unanimously hailed her the most engaging and talented young ingénue in living memory. She gave a good deal of her spare time to discouraging my determination to marry her.

Dulcy's Chicago premiere was the only time I ever sat in an orchestra seat at an opening of one of my plays. Being with Margalo made it an almost euphoric occasion. She and the audience laughed in spots that had been laughless in Indianapolis. When the curtain fell on the first act, Margalo and I went outside and moved about among the intermission smokers, looking for George. George did not appear. When the curtain fell on the second act we found Mr. Tyler in the lobby. He was beaming, indicating that he was not worrying about George or anything else. Margalo suggested that George might be backstage, so we trotted around to the stage door. No, the doorman said, he hadn't seen Mr. Kaufman all evening. None of the actors had either. We visited Lynn and the rest of the cast and found them exhilarated by the audience's acceptance of two-thirds of the play.

At last Margalo and I found George back in the theater's scene dock, leaning like a section of pipe against the wall. He was disconsolately looking at the floor, the fingers of one hand slowly and mechanically combing themselves through his thick, black hair. He was almost numb with despair.

"Well?" I asked.

"Well, not what you could really call well," George answered gloomily. "We've written ourselves a nice, high-type failure." I stared. "Why do you think so, George?" asked the astonished Margalo. "For one thing," said George, "it's over an hour too long." I answered, "George, it may be running ten minutes longer tonight than it did in Indianapolis, but the second act curtain has been down five minutes and in five minutes more it will be going up again." I looked at my watch. "We should ring down the final curtain about eleven ten. What the hell do you mean 'an hour too long'?"

"The show stinks," George murmured. I wondered if I were going out of my mind.

"George, it's a darling play," Margalo managed to say, "everybody loves it." George's grunt dismissed her childish nonsense. Now my concern had turned to exasperation. "God damn it, George, you're talking like an idiot. An hour too long! If it's even ten minutes too long, it's because of the new laughs. You can't deny there's been more laughter tonight than we had all last week." George clung grimly to his conviction of disaster.

"It's artificial," he said. That was when I learned that playwrights do not necessarily have the same immediate reactions to their first success. The next day George was quite himself again and completely reconciled to success. From then on, throughout our years together his rare dark moods were always validly objective.

Dulcy stayed in Chicago through the summer and was the first hit of the New York season when it opened on August 13 at the Frazee Theater on Forty-second Street near Eighth Avenue.

In my *Morning Telegraph* days, I had permitted myself two daily delights. One was listening to a single act of whatever was being sung at the Metropolitan Opera House. In those days the opera season under Gatti-Casazza lasted from October until April. It took me a year to hear the entire *Ring*. I became passionately fond of Wagner, and one summer was a one-man fan club following Friedrich Schorr all over Europe to hear his Wotan. I still feel that hearing him in the last act of *Die Walküre* was one of the great rewards of life.

My other constant joy was stopping backstage at the New Amsterdam or wherever else W. C. Fields might be playing, to spend a few minutes listening to the young, fresh version of what since has become one of America's legendary characters. Bill had reached stardom as a comic through his original skill as a juggler. Eventually, Ziegfeld headlined him in the Follies, but he didn't like Fields very much, having a basic antipathy to all comedians. Backstage in his dressing room, Bill had a private bar, to which newspapermen and other friends were welcome at all times. It was a great haven when Prohibition came along.

At midnight on January 15, 1920, the United States officially went dry, and simultaneously with the midnight chimes New York City's first speakeasy opened for business. For several days countless street doors had been fitted with peepholes and reinforced locks. Before the month was out it was evident that unless all five boroughs were leveled to the ground there was going to be no lack of alcoholic refreshment stands.

On January 17, 1920, newspapers reported that New York had dutifully accepted the noble experiment. In Washington, John Kramer, National Prohibition Administrator, stated, "No trouble is expected in enforcing the law. In most states our organization is perfect." He assured the country of his certainty that federal forces working with state and municipal authorities would quickly bring all lawbreakers to justice and that there would be "no difficulties in big cities like Chicago and New York." He also told us that prohibition directors in each state had ample manpower with which to control the legal uses of liquor—keeping track, for instance, of doctors' prescriptions (which by law would limit the purchase of spirituous drink by individual patients to one pint every ten days). Other headline stories included a jubilant announcement by the W.C.T.U. of an expansion of its activities. It now intended, it was reported, to make the whole world dry.

Possibly because of the snow-covered streets, New York's farewell to public drinking was less of a binge than the recent New Year's Eve spree. There was a good deal of noise in bars and bottle houses but remarkably little disorder and few arrests for drunkenness. Some of the big Broadway restaurants had conducted mock funeral services. Healy's staged a floor show, "The Death of Bacchus." "Auld Lang Syne" got full treatment in scores of places about to close their doors forever. There had been a spurt of last-minute buying. The cost of cocktails soared to one dollar each, and dealers got whatever they demanded for bottled goods. But the city-wide saturnalia that the police had been warned to expect did not occur. The average citizen had been too stunned to do more than lay in supplies.

The following Sunday's rotogravure sections depicted some of the alterations already undergone by familiar institutions. The bar in the old Waldorf-Astoria on Thirty-fourth Street was shown transformed into a candy shop with smiling salesgirls displaying dolls now on sale there. Other pictures showed saloons converted into laundries, hardware stores, real-estate offices, and soft-drink parlors.

Reaction had begun, however, and clear voices of protest were being raised. An editorial in the *World* contended that the Eighteenth Amendment in no way expressed a mandate of the people of America. The drys had achieved it not with popular support but by political connivance and intimidation. No opportunity had been given the nation's voters to express an objection at the polls. Bainbridge Colby, soon to be Woodrow Wilson's Secretary of State, angrily termed the Volstead Act "a fraudulent success." He added that the drys' behest to their opponents that they be good sports and accept the new law cheerfully was like being invited to smile by the thief who had picked your pocket.

There was news that enforcement had begun. Hundreds of cases of liquor not loaded on ships in time for legal export had been seized at city piers. The first arrest in Manhattan for an illegal sale of hard stuff was that of Michael Minden, long a respected saloon keeper. He was charged with selling a glass of brandy and was released under a thousand-dollar bond. I don't know what happened to Mr. Minden, but his defiance of the law did not immediately spearhead anything like a crusade of open resistance. Most bar owners took other steps. Hundreds went out of business. Others had moved the greater part of their stocks before the last day of grace and were opening their hideaways. At first, admittance was restricted to old and trustworthy customers, but before long the mention of a regular client's name usually enabled the first-timer to slake his thirst.

Midtown Manhattan had the greatest density of illegal oases. At one time you could be served in almost every building on West Fifty-second Street between Fifth and Sixth avenues. The prevalence of speaks was noted in the edition of the *Ziegfeld Follies* which came along in June.

When John Steel's usual silver-tenor tribute to the year's "Most Wonderful Girl in the World" ended on his usual high C and the lights dimmed out on Ben Ali Haggin's new tableau of Ziegfeld beauties, from the orchestra pit came an explosion of noises familiar to everyone in the audience, a raucous simulation of the concrete mixers, steam shovels, and riveting machines then engaged in the construction of the Broadway subway. As the sounds died away the curtain rose on a jungle of scaffolding and cross-walks like those most of us had clambered over that night to get to the theater. On an elevated clearing was W. C. Fields. Quiet, benign, he stood behind a whistling peanut roaster, courteously exchanging good evenings with a pass-ing policeman. When the cop had strolled into the wings, a man furtively approached the peanut stand. The dia-logue went pretty much like this:

FIELDS: "Seeking sustenance from peanuts, friend? Those small yet succulent morsels of tastiness?"

STRANGER: "Are you Harry?"

FIELDS: "Harry? I? What prompts you to ask if I am Harry?"

STRANGER: "I'm a friend of Charley Bates. He said just to mention his name."

FIELDS (gropingly): "Bates, Bates, Charley Bates? Chris-tened Charles, I presume?"

STRANGER: "Yes, sir. Of St. Joe."

FIELDS: "Of St. Joe, you say?"

STRANGER: "Yes, sir. He was here last month. Charles G. Bates."

FIELDS: "Ah! Charles G. Bates. A bell seems to tinkle. I concede the name might in truth be familiar. Perchance you too have a monicker?"

STRANGER: "Yes, sir. Gus Ferderber." (He offers a calling card, the surface of which Fields thumbs suspiciously.)

FIELDS: "You'll pardon me, I trust. Mountebanks could easily have such things printed in order to fleece honest mer-chants in the goober game."

STRANGER (tearfully): "But I *am* Gus Ferderber. I just got to town today."

FIELDS (doubtfully): "I see. And where is your permanent abode?"

STRANGER: "St. Joe."

FIELDS (cynically): "Come, come, now. Don't tell me there are *two* people in St. Joe."

STRANGER: "Honest. I've lived in St. Joe all my life."

FIELDS: "There's no need to whimper. Do you have anything to support your preposterous statement?" (The stranger removes his straw hat and lets Fields examine its inner band. Fields reads: "Joe Zilch. Gents' Furnishings. Paris, London, and St. Joe." He returns the hat and offers his hand.)

FIELDS: "'Tis clear you have not told a tissue of lies. I welcome you to our little settlement. Any friend of brother what'shisname—what *was* his name again?"

STRANGER: "Charley Bates."

FIELDS: "To be sure, to be sure. Old Charley Bates. As I was about to say, any friend of Charley Bates is a friend of Harry Musgrove Brandywine, Third. Just a second, Doc." (Fields presses a lever and the peanut roaster is transformed into a completely stocked bar.) "Name it, brother."

Despite frequent raids and padlockings the police were neighborly and made few arrests. I can remember sitting one evening in the Penwick—many speaks quickly became known by other than their owners' first names—when leisurely conversations at the tables were halted by an attention-getting rap of a bung-starter on the bar. A calm voice announced, "Finish your drinks, please, visitors." Drained glasses were hastily replaced by others half-filled with near-beer, lemonade, and other legal liquids. The removed glasses, with all the opened bottles behind the bar, were dropped through two automatically opened trap-doors. A minute later a pair of federal agents in civilian clothes entered through the unlocked street door and surveyed the room. Some of the glasses on the tables were sniffed, and there was a brief inspection of the bar's soda fountain supplies. Then the raiders left as quietly as they

had come, having made no descent into the subcellar
oubliette.

Protection was general. Most of the larger Manhattan
speaks, many of which catered to more than a thousand
customers each day, never suffered a single interruption in
operation. At five o'clock every afternoon on one end of
the bar of the Mansion, on Forty-first Street off Madison
Avenue, one could see a hundred setups for old-fashioneds
alone, ready for the cocktail-hour rush.

Many New Yorkers depended on home deliveries by
bootleggers for their domestic drinking. "Al's here," cried
a character in Don Marquis's *The Old Soak*, giving a
decade one of its most popular bywords. In the early days
of Prohibition many of us were supplied with trustworthy wines and whiskies by stewards from the ocean
liners. But before long the real stewards were augmented
by impostors with questionable wares. "But it's right off
the ship," protested the bogus steward in a current joke. "I
don't doubt," agreed his client. "Scraped off."

For a while, the dubious origin of available supplies
stimulated residential manufacture. "Leslie Hanger's new
home'll have three bathrooms," said Kin Hubbard in one
of his daily newspaper comments on the American scene.
"One for beer, one for gin, an' one for Saturday."
Throughout the years of Prohibition thousands of American householders became good wine makers and were able
to get enough pure alcohol, oil of coriander, and other in-
gredients to make decent gin.

Dr. Walter Damrosch brewed the best beer in New
York in the rear of his big house on East Seventy-first

Street, using recipes brought to America by his German ancestors. Every Saturday night at least a score of friends, mostly musicians, would arrive for buffet supper and after a night of music, mirth, and Munchener go home to the sound of church bells. A half-dozen servants were assisted by Mrs. Damrosch and the five Damrosch daughters in keeping plates and glasses filled. Georges Barrère, America's greatest flutist, would tell inimitable stories about musicians, and Chaliapin might treat us to the defiance scene from *Mephistophele*.

The commodious cellars of many advantaged citizens had been so well stocked before Prohibition that they and their guests enjoyed the finest wines, whiskies, and other beverages until bootlegging and the Volstead Act died together.

The increasing strength of gangsters was becoming a public concern, yet several of the more affluent hoodlums opened opulent places that attracted decent people who were unaware of their ownership. At the same time, there were establishments run by men of probity. Such people as Jim Moriarty managed not only to withstand the competition of the underworld but won friends and admiration that did not desert them when the death of the Volstead Act allowed them to become legitimate businessmen again. Jack Kriendler and Charley Burns had to change their secret places of business several times, but when the Twenty-first Amendment—Repeal—came along, they were already established among New York's foremost restaurateurs and their 21 Club had become a national institution.

Of all the places that offered entertainment along with food and booze, the one I remember best and most affectionately was the Club Durant, which flourished under the bend of the Sixth Avenue El on Fifty-third Street. Festivities there never got under way until after midnight. Then Jimmy Durante, with his partners Lou Clayton and Eddie Jackson, would convulse as many as could be crowded into a former second-story loft, until the hour of dawn. Now and then, widely known figures from the entertainment world would volunteer comic turns, but it was Durante and his crew who filled the place.

Jimmy had everyone in his pocket singing such great songs as "I'm Jimmy the Well-dressed Man" with its memorable "I jest got off de steamship Miewritania" and "I kin git along without Broadway but kin Broadway git along without me?" Invariably after the first few bars he would scream in frustration "Stop de music! You're roonin' de material!" and throw his battered hat at the orchestra. There was that great skit laid in an opium den: Eddie Jackson, a wretched hophead, lay in a corner, while Jimmy, a sinister ruler of the underworld, received a report on the den's business from Lou Clayton, its manager. What howls of laughter were heard after Jackson dared to interrupt with an inoffensive greeting to the vice king. Jimmy would glare at Jackson with lethal malevolence, then hesitate as his hand whisked to a back pants' pocket. "No!" he would say, "why go to my hip for a rat like dat?" Then there was the "Shipwrecked" skit, with Jimmy going mad with thirst as the trio sat on an imaginary raft in an ocean of waste. "Dis suspense is deefening," Jimmy would moan. Then a moment later he would cry, "Land! Land!" "It ain't land, Jimmy," Clayton would tell him gently. "You're just slowly going mad with the monotony. What you see is just the horizon." "Den pull for it," Jimmy would shout. "It's better than nothin'."

Just as the best-paid chefs presided in the kitchens of the better wet spots, so did star talent from the theater become part of their floor shows. At the Sutton Club you could hear Beatrice Lillie; Fred and Adele Astaire danced at the Trocadero, and Libby Holman sang her blues at the Lido. I shall never forget Helen Morgan, sitting atop a piano, brokenheartedly singing "Why Was I Born?" to the more raffish crowds in Dutch Schultz's Embassy Club.

Some of the gangster-owned places went out of business because of internal trouble, not federal padlocks. One night in The Club Abbey, a popular hangout for the racketeer elite, a fracas grew from the playful antics of some relaxing hoods. There were a couple of bursts of gunfire, two or three patrons were wounded by bullets, and in the ensuing melee the club's glassware and furnishings were pretty well destroyed. The papers made quite a story of the incident, but as soon as the joint was redecorated, it opened again under a different name. About the same time, Jack "Legs" Diamond, another gangland notable, participated in a shooting affair at The Hotsy-Totsy which resulted in two actual and several near-deaths.

Undoubtedly the brassiest night clubs were those in which "Texas" Guinan was mistress of ceremonies. Occasionally her clubs had to change their address, but they were always filled, not only with noisy, heavy spenders, but with people of culture and repute. When federal agents arrived to close one of her headquarters two United States Senators were among the annoyed but unruffled patrons.

As Prohibition entered its fourteenth year, its failure was at last officially admitted. State after state, with Utah

7 2

the last, ratified the Twenty-first Amendment, which would bring Repeal. On December 5, 1933, the long foolishness was over.

Overnight, flask-canes became curious. Rum Row off Montauk Point was reported down to six vessels now able to make legal entries to port. Marquis James says Janssen's Restaurant received the first new license. The branch of the Childs chain next to the Paramount Theater must have been almost next in line because the papers next day said six members of Childs board of directors were present to watch the ministrations of four newly hired bartenders. The forty-thousand existing permits to deal in industrial alcohol were relinquished by the majority of their holders. Ocean liners used to being swamped with business when their bars opened on outbound voyages found an equal surge of passengers as they approached New York. The papers said the first man with an admissible bottle got off the *Monarch of Bermuda*. I returned from Europe that same day on the *Majestic*. I wasn't empty-handed either. And I know the man from Bermuda couldn't have felt more like celebrating than I did.

Merrymaking, however, was not our exclusive occupation during those years. Because of our success with *Dulcy*, Tyler again turned to George Kaufman and me to supply a fresh vehicle for his youngest star, Helen Hayes. Helen had captured the town with her performance of the imaginary daughter of William Gillette in one outstanding scene in James Barrie's *Dear Brutus*. Her first play under the Tyler banner had been *Golden Days*. Except for Helen's performance and that of a young British new-

comer named Leslie Howard, *Golden Days* received bad
notices and died quickly. George and I locked ourselves
up and within a week had the basis of a story we both
liked. Helen would play the young, gently bred wife of a
not-too-bright piano salesman. Through her help and encouragement he would be one of two candidates being
considered for an important executive position. The successful candidate was to be announced following a banquet at which both men would make speeches. Helen's
husband would rely on a selection from *One Hundred
Speeches for All Occasions*. And, when his rival would be
called on first, he would make the same speech Helen's
husband had memorized. With her spouse in a state of collapse, she would rise, apologize for his sudden attack of
laryngitis, announce that she knows what he had intended
to say, and clinch the job with a modest and winning im-
provisation. George and I felt it would furnish a good part
for Helen and would allow some fun with the stuffy
smugness becoming more and more puncturable in American business.

After Tyler had approved the outline of the story,
George and I went down to the apartment near Gramercy
Park where Miss Hayes and her mother were living.
Helen, although she had never lived farther south than
Washington, liked the idea of playing a southern belle: we
had decided that the wily little husband booster would be
more amusing if she operated with guileless honeysuckle-
and-corn-pone speech.

"At one point," we told her, "when you are entertaining the boss and his wife we want you to sing a couple
of spirituals. Do you play the piano?"

"Oh, yes," said Helen.

7 4

The door had hardly closed behind us when Helen was on the telephone ordering a piano, engaging a teacher for a crash instruction course, and making an appointment for her first singing lesson.

George was now drama editor of the *Times*. Assured that *Dulcy* would have a long run, I had given up my job on the *Telegraph*, but George liked the security offered by the *Times* against possibly rainy days, and he held the post until we had written half a dozen successes. In his dual role of playwright-editor, George bewildered and infuriated managers, press agents, and stars connected with our plays. They were obliged to accept his self-imposed restraint against showing favoritism in his columns to any play in which he had a personal concern. Our own press agents were forever bewailing that anything but a Kaufman–Connelly show could get fair representation in the theatrical section of the *Times*.

Before the opening of *To the Ladies*, our new play, George was reproached by its press agent for the meager linage he had given it. George's scruples had made him reject a story about Helen Hayes the press agent had submitted for advance publicity.

"For God's sake, George!" complained the rebuffed press agent, "what do I have to do to get your own star's name in the paper?"

"Shoot her," said George.

One day George took with him the completed rough draft of the second act of *To the Ladies*, to read on the way to his office. He put in a long day at the *Times*, got home well after midnight, and discovered he had left the script in the subway. It was our only copy, and we had planned to go over it the next morning. George appeared on time that day, though a little bleary-eyed. When I failed to discover anything odd about the script, he confessed. He had sat up most of the night retyping the act from memory.

Rochester was a popular tryout town, and *To the Ladies* was taken there for its dress rehearsal and first public performance. Tyler was not a man who wasted money on what he considered unessential items in a production. Lynn Fontanne had corrected his belief that costumes, particularly those of leading ladies, could be picked up cheaply. I think he lost quite a bit of blood when she let him know that *Dulcy's* dresses had to come from Bouet Soeurs, then about the top in *haute couture*. He became reconciled to her insistence when he saw the difference between her selections and the junk he had expected her to wear.

Scenery was another area for Tyler economy. *Dulcy* had only one set, but a great many stage directions had had to be changed to accommodate its entrances and exits to walls, stairways, ceilings, etc., assembled from half a dozen ancient productions. For years Tyler kept on a wall in his office a sketch I made of the Nutley, New Jersey, living room as seen from backstage. There were only slight exaggerations in my reproduction of the scenery constructor's stencils on the backs of flats and wings: HEART OF MARYLAND, ACT I, L. 3; UNCLE TOM'S CABIN, ACT II, CENTER; BEN HUR, ACT III, SCENE 4, and so on.

I don't know where someone had found the shades for the wall-bracket lights in Helen's parlor in *To the Ladies*. I first saw them on the afternoon before the dress rehearsal. George agreed with me that they had come from one of the earliest stage sets to be lighted by electricity. That night, when rehearsal ended, Tyler turned to the back of the house where George and I were sitting, "O.K. with you, boys?," expecting the customary approval of the authors.

"Not quite," I called back. "Eddie!" The stage manager came on the set. "Would you change those bracket-lamp shades for the ones I gave you?"

Tyler gaped uncomprehendingly as Eddie removed the antiques and substituted a plausible set of shades I had bought that afternoon at the Five and Ten.

"With our compliments," I said. "Now the room looks as if human beings lived there."

Tyler looked heavenward and dramatically slapped a hand to his forehead.

"My God," he roared, "another Clyde Fitch!"

Fitch was America's most demanding playwright. Nevertheless the lampshades stayed, and when a few months later a second company went on the road, exact duplicates were provided. We knew that *To the Ladies* would be a success, and at the calls for "author" at the opening we had the gall to ring the curtain up on two clothing store dummies. The audience thought it was very clever of us.

Another, and quite different type of producer was David Belasco. He, Alec Woollcott said, "like a true artist, never considers financial cost and works till he drops, trying to realize what he is after. It's a pity he doesn't have a medium."

Because of his artistic pretentiousness, David Belasco was the butt of many critics. At the same time everyone respected his talent as a showman. The stage decor of his plays offered photographic realism other producers have never surpassed. Years before he presented David Warfield in *The Merchant of Venice*, he began acquiring authentic seventeenth-century Italian furniture and *objets d'art* to use in the production. His search for anything that might add to its pictorial validity became well known to art dealers. There was a report that when Belasco brought a pre-*Merchant* production to Boston for its tryout, a temporary antique shop was opened next door to the theater because his patronage was so valuable. Unhappily, when Warfield's Shylock finally came to life, the performance of the play received less attention than its embellishments and it died of opulence.

A highly successful and less costly achievement graced his production of *The Governor's Lady*. One scene was in a contemporary Childs restaurant. Besides the faithful reproduction of the restaurant's tables, chairs, and tiled walls, when the curtain rose two Childs cooks were making real pancakes on real griddles which wafted confirming aromas into the nostrils of audiences.

I once was privileged to admire at close hand another bit of Belasco realism. Before the curtain rose on a dress rehearsal of *Lulu Belle*, which Charles MacArthur and Edward Sheldon had written for Leonore Ulric, Belasco invited me backstage to see the setting of the first act. With his gently hesitant speech—his stress of sibilants often made him seem to be lisping—he said:

"I wanted you to ssee what I have att-emp-ted to do before I raisse the curtain. Once it'ss up the action

mountss sso sswiftly you won't be able to apprecciate the
sset. Sso feasst your eyess."

The exteriors of a Harlem movie theater, a poolroom,
and other buildings had been meticulously achieved. I con-
gratulated Belasco on the details. When I stopped he was
reproachful.

"You didn't notisse something I'm particularly proud
of." He led me across the stage to the curb of a sidewalk
and with glowing pride said:

"Issn't that the God-damnedesst realesst fireplug you
ever ssaw in your life?"

And indeed it was.

With two hits on Broadway, George and I began
serious consideration of an idea both of us had found
stimulating. We would write an ironic comedy about a
tired, blasé New York playwright who goes back to the
small middlewestern town of his birth to reembrace the
simplicities of life his years in the city had made him
forget. The fun was to come from his discovering that
bucolic Millersville had changed since he had left and with
its country club, urban night life, and other innovations,
was now as sophisticated as New York. At first we called
the play *Little Old Millersville*, later we changed it to *West
of Pittsburgh*, and when it reached New York, it was *The
Deep Tangled Wildwood*. While writing it, George and I
told ourselves that luck had had much to do with the success of *Dulcy* and *To the Ladies*. So we decided not to get
too cocky over our talents. On every detail in the new play
we would seek the comment and advice of more experienced people and thus minimize the likelihood of error. We

listened to anyone for whom we had respect. I like to think that what happened to *The Deep Tangled Wildwood* was due to our attack of humility, rather than to Messrs. Kaufman and Connelly.

Denman Maley, a comedian whose talents America never had a chance to appreciate because of his early death, was wonderfully funny as a radio announcer bored to death with broadcasting, which was then in its infancy. Shortly after the play closed, New York managers received the following engraved notification:

MRS. DENMAN MALEY
ANNOUNCES
THE IDLENESS OF HER HUSBAND
DENMAN

It brought more offers of work than Denman had ever before received.

Our play quickly faded from the public memory, but the title stayed alive in the words of Irving Berlin's popular "Lazy." If you ever sang

I wanna peep through the deep tangled wildwood,
Counting sheep 'til I sleep like a child would,

you may have thought Berlin had Samuel Woodworth in mind.

The world in which we moved was small, but it was churning with a dynamic group of young people who included Robert C. Benchley, Robert S. Sherwood, Ring Lardner, Dorothy Parker, Franklin P. Adams, Heywood

Broun, Edna Ferber, Alice Duer Miller, Harold Ross, Jane Grant, Frank Sullivan, and Alexander Woollcott. We were together constantly. One of the habitual meeting places was the large studio of New York's preeminent magazine illustrator, Marjorie Moran McMein, of Muncie, Indiana. On the advice of a numerologist, she concocted a new first name when she became a student at the Chicago Art Institute. Neysa McMein. Neysa's studio on the northeast corner of Sixth Avenue and Fifty-seventh Street was crowded all day by friends who played games and chatted with their startingly beautiful young hostess as one pretty girl model after another posed for the pastel head drawings that would soon delight the eyes of America on the covers of such periodicals as the *Ladies' Home Journal, Cosmopolitan, The American* and *The Saturday Evening Post.*

At times every newsstand sparkled with half a dozen of Neysa's beauties. Any afternoon at her studio you might encounter Jascha Heifetz, the violin prodigy, now grown up and beginning his adult career; Arthur Samuels, composer and wit who was soon to collaborate with Fritz Kreisler on the melodious operetta *Apple Blossoms* and a few years later became managing editor of *The New Yorker*; Janet Flanner, blazing with personality, later, over several decades, a journalistic legend as Genêt, Paris correspondent of *The New Yorker*; and John Peter Toohey, a gentle free-lance press agent, deeply loved by everyone who ever crossed his path. Toohey wrote stories for *The Saturday Evening Post* and collaborated on a successful comedy entitled *Swifty.* John was the acknowledged founder of the Thanatopsis Inside Straight Literary and Chowder Club and a target of many harmless practical jokes. One would also see Sally Farnham, the sculptress, whose studio was in the same building. Today one of her great works stands almost around the corner from her old workshop. It is the heroic equestrian statue of Simón Bolívar at the Sixth Avenue entrance to Central Park. Another habituée was the most photographed society beauty of that time, the beautiful Julia Hoyt. Among Neysa's noteworthy full-figure portraits in oil were those of Julia and Janet Flanner.

There was always a cluster of young actresses. Margalo and Ruth Gillmore, Winifred Lenihan, Tallulah Bankhead, Myra Hampton, and Lenore Ulric. Despite the near-bedlam about her, Neysa's eyes never left her work. At the end of a day and the completion of another delicately executed magazine cover, Neysa's smock and face would be smeared with chalk and paint. She would disappear and five minutes later rejoin us fresh as a flower, ready to listen, entertain, and be entertained. After five o'clock the big studio would be crowded with her cronies, many engaged in daily sessions of poker, crap, backgammon, and cribbage. Samuels or someone else would be at the piano.

Before *The Deep Tangled Wildwood* vanished, George and I were starting on a new venture. For the second time I had found a story in *The Saturday Evening Post* I wanted to dramatize. It was *Merton of the Movies* by Harry Leon Wilson. It told of a guileless youth to whom movies were the only important thing in life and Hollywood was a holy city. He believed everything he read in the fan magazines and decided to seek a career in

Hollywood. In spite of constant misadventures and frequent disillusionments he emerged on top of the acting heap with most of his naive ideals intact. George liked the story too, and Tyler obtained the dramatic rights from Wilson.

Even before we began work on the adaptation Tyler had signed a young man who proved to be the ideal Merton. He was Glenn Hunter, whom Broadway had seen before briefly in Percy MacKaye's touching poetic fantasy *The Scarecrow*. We told Tyler the play would require an unusually large investment in scenery. One scene would show the filming of a ship at sea during a violent storm. To our astonishment Tyler blandly said, "It sounds great. Go right ahead, boys." Hugh Ford was engaged as director. Today, most newspaper drama departments report on plays' out-of-town tryouts, but *Merton* was able to open in Brooklyn with no journalistic visitors from Manhattan. While *Merton* started its pre-New York road tour, George and I were able to turn to a project we'd been intermittently assembling for months, a new kind of intimate review inspired by a production called *No, Sirree*.

The *Chauve Souris*, a potpourri of Russian variety acts with the great Balieff as master of ceremonies, was the latest importation of Morris Gest, David Belasco's son-in-law and an early-day Hurok. One of its highlights was a new dance, "The March of the Wooden Soldiers," whose music will probably never lose its popularity. Someone suggested that it might be fun to take over the Forty-ninth Street Theater on a night when the *Chauve Souris* was not playing and stage an evening's entertainment whipped up for our own amusement and presented to an invited audience of friends. It was loosely patterned after the Russian production and called, with an acknowledged minimum of wit, the *No, Sirree.* The news of our plan reached H. T. Parker, the dean of Boston's drama critics, and prompted him to make a special trip to New York to see it. He found the program itself interesting enough to reproduce it in the Boston *Transcript.* Here is a copy:

NO, SIRREE!
An Anonymous Entertainment by the Vicious Circle
of the Hotel Algonquin
49TH STREET THEATRE
SUNDAY EVENING, APRIL 30TH, 1922
(Theatre by Courtesy of the Messrs. Shubert)

Spirit of the American Drama .... Heywood Broun

OPENING CHORUS
Alexander Woollcott, John Peter Toohey,
Robert C. Benchley, George S. Kaufman,
Marc Connelly and Franklin P. Adams

"THE EDITOR REGRETS——"
Mabel Cenci .... Marc Connelly, '25
George Medeci .... J. M. Kerrigan, '26
A Composer-Author .... Donald Ogden Stewart, '25
Dante .... Harold Gould, '28
An Average Male Reader .... Henry Wise Miller, '22
An Average Female Reader .... Mary Brandon, '30
Venice at the time of Dante. The editorial offices of
"Droll Tales," a popular twice-a-month magazine
which flourished at that period

THE FILMLESS MOVIES
Baron Ireland and F. P. A.

THE GREASY HAG
An O'Neill Play in One Act

The Road to New York

CAST
(In the order of appearance)
Elizabeth Inchcape, known as Coal-Barge Bessie,
a retired water-front prostitute ... John Peter Toohey
The Murdered Woman .... Ruth Gillmore
First Agitated Seaman .... George S. Kaufman
Second Agitated Seaman .... Alexander Woollcott
Third Agitated Seaman .... Marc Connelly
Scene
Vote for One Backroom of Billy the Bishop's saloon,
near Coentie's Slip, New York
Firemen's forecastle on a freighter bound east from Rio.
Time—The present
Incidental music by Arthur H. Samuels

HE WHO GETS FLAPPED
With Robert E. Sherwood and the following ingenues:
June Walker, Winifred Lenihan, Juliet St. John-
Brenon, Tallulah Bankhead, Mary Kennedy, Ruth
Gillmore, Lenore Ulric, Helen Hayes and Mary
Brandon.

BETWEEN THE ACTS
The Manager .... Brock Pemberton
The Manager's Brother .... Murdock Pemberton
And the following first nighters: Dorothy Parker, Alice
Duer Miller, Neysa McMein, Beatrice Kaufman, Jane
Grant, Heywood Broun, Alexander Woollcott, Robert
C. Benchley, George S. Kaufman, Marc Connelly, Kel-
cey Allen, Arthur Bachrach.

"JOHNNY WEAVER," a Ballad
Sung by Reinald Werrenrath

BIG CASINO IS LITTLE CASINO
A Samuel Shipman Play
(*In Three Acts*)
James W. Archibald (a Rich Man) .. John Peter Toohey
Dregs (a Butler) .... Alexander Woollcott

Mr. Harper (a Broker) .... J. M. Kerrigan
John Findlay (a Young Attorney) .. George S. Kaufman
O'Brien (a Detective) .... Franklin P. Adams
Margaret (Archibald's Daughter) ...... Mary Kennedy
A Convict .... Marc Connelly
The Broker's Boy .... David H. Wallace
The Governor of New York ..... Robert E. Sherwood
Guests ... Alice Duer Miller, Neysa McMein, Jane Grant

Synopsis of Scenes

ACT   I—The Home of James W. Archibald
ACT   II—The same. A week later
ACT   III—A Wall Street Office. Two days later
Offstage Music by J. Heifetz

INTERMISSION

MARC CONNELLY
"That Somewhat Different Cornettist"
—in—
"A NIGHT AT FRANK CAMPBELL'S"
Scene—Frank Campbell's   Time—Night

ZOWIE
Or The Curse of an Akins Heart
(*A Romanza In One Act*)
"Nor all your piety and wit"—*From the Persian*
CAST
(In the order of appearance)
Marmaduke LaSalle
(a Stomach Specialist) .... John Peter Toohey
Lady friend of LaSalle's .... Neysa McMein
Another lady friend of LaSalle's .... Louise Closser Hale
Dindo (a Wandering Busboy) .... J. M. Kerrigan
Zhoolie Venable
(a Suppressed Desire*) .... Ruth Gillmore
* Suppressed in Humansville, Mo.,
sometime in April, 1908.

8 6

Mortimer Van Loon
(a Decayed Gentleman) .... George S. Kaufman
Archibald Van Alstyne
(a Precisionist) .... Alexander Woollcott
Lemuel Pip (an Old Taxi Driver) ...... Harold W. Ross
Scene—A Capitol Lunch. Time—Printemps, 1922.
Offstage Music by J. Heifetz

MR. WHIM PASSES BY
An A. A. Milne Play

Cynthia .... Helen Hayes
Nigel .... Sidney Blackmer
Uncle Tertius .... J. M. Kerrigan
The scene is the morning room at The Acacias,
Wipney-cum-Chiselickwick

SONG: "KAUFMAN AND CONNELLY
FROM THE WEST"

BEATRICE HERFORD
—in—
"The Algonquin Girl"

FINALE
by the entire company
Golden Ptg. Service, N.Y.

Skits such as "Big Casino Is Little Casino," "Mr. Whim Passes By," and "The Greasy Hag" were travesties of plays written in the manner of Samuel Shipman, A. A. Milne, and Eugene O'Neill. A "Big Casino Is Little Casino" program note read, "Offstage music by J. Heifetz." To keep Jascha in his place we didn't even allow him to come onstage for a bow. George wrote the travesty and

8 7

filled it with Shipman's hyperelegant language. In the opening scene Alice Duer Miller and Neysa appeared as typical Shipman society women.

"What a beautiful drawing room. It is replete with antique works of art," purred Neysa.

"Yes," said Alice, "it reminds me of one of which I read in a volume."

Heywood Broun played the chubby Balieff, his great bulk resembling the physical appearance of the Russian. Heywood could never find time to be dapper. His usual appearance made someone compare him to an unmade bed. Another identified him as a one-man slum.

Robert Benchley had promised to furnish a skit for the show but had failed to deliver it. For that reason his name was omitted from the program. The night before the performance he improvised a monologue, "The Treasurer's Report," an appeal for funds for a nebulous charitable organization, which his stumbling self-conscious treasurer never got around to identifying. It was the highlight of the evening. When the cheers following Benchley's first theatrical appearance died down, Broun, as Balieff, explained that while Mr. Benchley had been a bit too nervous to name the charity he had in mind, he assumed most of the audience knew it was for The National Fund to Retire The William A. Brady Scenery. Everyone present knew that William A. Brady, who put on at least a half-dozen plays every year, like George Tyler, did not believe in wasting money on stage decor. He had an octagonal library set everyone had seen at least ten times. Even when it was becoming shabby it served as a reception room in the White House in John Farrar and Stephen Vincent Benét's *The Awful Mrs. Eaton*. Stung by Broun's comment, the next year at the Park Theater, Brady proudly waded through a surf of tulles and silk gauze at the conclusion of the first performance of his opulent production of the Capek brothers' *Insect Comedy* to announce:

"Last year there was a certain amateur show—I didn't see it, but Grace George [Brady's wife] told me that the big joke of the evening was a reference to the Brady scenery. This is my apology." Then he wove his way offstage, a bit stewed but more than reconciled to having spent a fortune on the production.

Other than H. T. Parker's *Transcript* the only paper that offered a critique of *No, Sirree* was *The New York Times*. The comment on the show was written by Laurette Taylor, substituting for Alexander Woollcott, the *Times*'s official critic, who had made his own debut as an actor in *No, Sirree*. Laurette rolled up her sleeves and with serious gusto panned hell out of everyone connected with *No, Sirree*.

No, Sirree had contained so much fun that George and I decided New York was ready for a professional production of a new kind of revue. The small Punch and Judy theater on Forty-ninth Street, where Charles Hopkins had staged a miniature but enchanting *Treasure Island*, seemed just right for what we were concocting. Because of the location of the theater we decided to call the revue *The Forty-Niners*. We invited a dozen of our friends to contribute sketches.

We turned first to Ring Lardner. Ring had begun to put down on paper the extemporaneous nonsense plays he recited to enraptured listeners at his house in Great Neck. You can find several of them still sparkling in anthologies of his work. "The Tridget of Greva" was elaborated a bit for its first stage presentation in *The Forty-Niners*. The setting for "The Tridget" consisted of a row of three skiffs, each containing a lone fisherman. The men weren't exactly fishing. J. M. Kerrigan had half a dozen lines over the side to which he paid no attention as he exchanged bits of staccato talk with Roland Young and Sidney Toler. Kerrigan had arrived with Dublin's Abbey Theatre Company on its first visit to America and been engaged to play the Shadow in Molnar's *Liliom*. Philip Moeller, directing the play for the recently formed Theater Guild, was addicted to precious delicacies of expression in his instructions to the cast. Kerrigan had no stomach for Moeller's hyper-sensitivity but listened patiently as Moeller coined a new subtlety in directorial communication. Interrupting a scene Kerrigan was rehearsing with another actor, Moeller said:

"Joe, would you repeat that last line?" Joe did. "Excellent. Now could you possibly read it with a bit more of a pear-shaped tone?" Joe winced inwardly.

"Of course, Philip. And which end of the pear would you like to have first?"

But back to "The Tridget." Roland Young had no fish pole. He sat in his boat with arms folded as if defying the world to make him fish. Sidney Toler sat with a bag of golf clubs, presumably prepared for a game in case his boat came to rest on a first tee. One of the most informative bits of its dialogue was this:

TOLER: "Where was you born?"
KERRIGAN: "Out of wedlock."
TOLER: "Mighty pretty country around there."

One of the early drafts of *The Tridget* called for each actor in turn to say, "I'd like some broth," with Lardner's stage direction: "They exit to a brothel." *The Tridget*'s big moment came when a Western Union messenger, apparently walking on water, brought Toler a telegram. The messenger waited while Toler opened the envelope and scanned the message.

"Any answer?" asked the messenger.

Toler stood up, blazing with wrath. "Yes!" he shouted, slapping the messenger's face. "*That's* my answer!"

The messenger was unruffled. "I see," he said thoughtfully, and walked away.

Dorothy Parker and Robert Benchley created what was described in the program as a one-act historical drama called "Nero." It began with the conversations of two Gardes Populaire on patrol duty during the French Revolution. The opening lines were memorable:

FIRST GARDE POPULAIRE: "As you know, Citoyen, this is the month of Thermidor and the Place Louis Quatorze is running with blood. What do you make of it all?"

SECOND GARDE POPULAIRE: "Only time will tell."

Throughout the action a red-robed Cardinal Richelieu sat on a throne far upstage, occasionally looking up from his game of solitaire to make such profound observations as "Many a mickle makes a muckle, but only God can make real maple syrup." And when a final offstage cry of "The Giants have won the pennant!" was heard, Grant and Lee entered and surrendered their swords to each other.

Those in the first-night audience who were completely receptive to what we were offering were in the minority. Few New Yorkers were brighter or more urbane than Frank Crowninshield, editor of *Vanity Fair* magazine. When he came backstage after the opening he wore a puzzled look. "Maybe I missed the point," he confessed, "but was it all supposed to be taking place in an insane asylum?"

Actually, the revue had a specific problem. Tyler had insisted that as a commère we employ May Irwin, the veteran comedienne, whose hearty, boisterous style was decades behind the avant-garde entertainment we were trying to produce. Tyler realized that *The Forty-Niners* was unlikely to survive the chill of its first-night reception but that if it did, Miss Irwin was the show's biggest anachronism and would have to be immediately replaced.

"By whom?" George and I asked simultaneously.

"One of you fellows. You were both pretty funny in *No, Sirree.*"

George refused point-blank. He had protested May Irwin's presence from the first and was both depressed and angry. He said he could be of more use making up the next Sunday's *Times* drama page. I said I'd go on for a couple of nights on condition that, if the business encouraged it, a professional comedian would take over. I went on as compère that night and said some of the lines Miss Irwin had decided were too unamusing to speak. Their gist was that since New York's theatergoers had proved themselves so hospitable to the current invasion of plays and players from Russia, Italy, Ireland, France, Germany, and Japan, we thought they might welcome a little group of American players presenting an entertainment depicting folkways of the United States. I then introduced the first number, a traditional folk dance from the Middle West performed annually during April and May in rural communities that marked the vernal change from heavy to light underwear. It was called "The Dance of the Small-Town Mayors," and the six funny fellows who clowned its primitive choreography had the audience laughing immediately.

The climate for the rest of the evening was much warmer than the night before, and as I was at least tolerable as master of ceremonies, the show had, to some degree, an outline of personality. We hadn't found anybody to take my place when *Merton of the Movies* opened around the corner on Forty-eighth Street at the Cort Theater. *Merton* had been running two weeks before I was able to see a performance. When the last curtain fell that night I went backstage to congratulate the cast. Glenn Hunter had become the talk of the town as Merton and was pretty proprietary about his new vehicle. As we shook hands he asked, "By the way, how's *your* show doing?"

By 1922, the year *Merton* came to town, lunch at the Round Table of the Algonquin Hotel had become institutional. The coterie that made up Round Table regulars numbered almost twenty, but more than eight or nine seldom would eat simultaneously. The magnetic influence that had brought us together at the Algonquin had been the personality of Frank Case, the hotel's legendary proprietor. Case had begun his career as a bellboy at the Algonquin and over the years had proved himself so dedicated and valuable that he had been made manager in his thirties. His personality was pretty well implied in a remark attributed to John Barrymore. Shortly after moving to New York from his home in Philadelphia he encountered a friend on Broadway. "Where are you staying?" he was asked. Barrymore said, "At a little place on Forty-fourth Street called the Algonquin." "Is it comfortable?" "It's wonderful," said Barrymore, "the fellow who runs it—his name is Case—is one of the most generous men in the world. He'd give you his shirt. This is it."

Generosity truly was a part of Frank's nature. During the twenties, many a hungry actor enjoyed his room and meals on credit until a job turned up. There was a story of a young married couple, newcomers to the hotel, who ate a meager Christmas-night dinner of cheese and crackers in their room, not knowing that the dining rooms downstairs were filled with other guests enjoying the turkey and plum pudding banquet that was served every Thanksgiving and Christmas with the compliments of the hotel. During Case's long years as a boniface one would often see a dozen or more Salvation Army uniforms in the hotel's two dining rooms. Case never explained that their presence was due partly to their having to pay only half of what everyone else did.

The Round Table had its beginning when Alec Woollcott, Harold Ross, F.P.A., and Jane Grant, her Y.M.C.A. duties ended, came back from France at the end of the war. The three men had all been on the editorial staff of *Stars & Stripes*. Woollcott had been blithely unconcerned about danger at the front. A dozen times in trenches under fire he had to be pulled back to comparative safety. F.P.A. and Ross had spent most of their service at their editorial desks in Paris, but Ross did have one experience of being under fire in odd circumstances. The big original Ferris wheel, built for the 1900 exposition, had been operating throughout the war. One afternoon Ross climbed into one of the Ferris wheel cars to look at a panorama of the city, expecting to be back on the ground within a few minutes. Something caused the wheel to stop, and Ross was suspended at the top of the structure for well over an hour—the same hour that the Germans chose to acquaint Paris with the existence of Big Bertha. From that night thereafter, the seventy-five-mile range cannon shells exploded haphazardly about Paris every hour for several weeks.

Jane Grant married Ross, and was back at her old job of society reporter on the *Times*. This quartet, with John Peter Toohey, augmented by Hawley Truax, another *Stars and Striper*, became daily frequenters of a corner table. By 1920 the expansion of the group had caused Case to reserve for its members the big round table at the rear of the larger dining room, which, because its habitués enjoyed one another's company so much, soon provoked envy and often malicious slander among outsiders who could not tolerate its gaiety. By 1921 the fellowship of the Round Table had burst into full flower. Its members, besides those already named, included: Brock Pemberton, about to produce the brilliant comedy *Enter Madame*; Murdock, his brother; beautiful Peggy Wood, whose voice was making her internationally known in musical plays; John V. A. Weaver, the poet, whom Peggy later married; Margaret Leech, fresh from Vassar, soon to be collaborating with Heywood Broun on their biography of

Anthony Comstock; Kate Sproehnle, an attractive free-lance journalist; Frank Sullivan, the humorist, and Ruth Hale.

Ruth Hale was a tireless champion of lost causes. The good writing with which she trumpeted Arthur Hopkins' plays revealed a lively, highly intelligent mind. In her private world she was an ardent feminist. She founded the Lucy Stone League dedicated to the protection of woman's individuality. Among its insistences were that married women be permitted to retain their maiden names. Jane Grant, Janet Flanner, Fola LaFollette, and Freda Kirchwey were among those who became resolute members. "A rolling stone gathers no boss," said George Kaufman. Heywood Broun heartily agreed with Ruth's principles. When anyone addressed her as "Mrs. Broun" after they were married he or she was emphatically told that that was not her name. For years Ruth conducted a one-woman war with the State Department, which, because of her marital status, refused to issue a passport to Ruth Hale. Eventually she was told that she could have a passport issued to "Mrs. Heywood Broun (known as Ruth Hale.)" She continued to forgo leaving the United States. When her young son, Heywood Hale Broun, was recuperating from an illness in a school in California, Ruth decided to assure herself of his recovery by visiting him. Expecting Ruth to telephone him in New York about the boy's progress, Heywood was concerned when after five days he had not heard from her. He telephoned the school but was told that she had not arrived. The next day he received a telegram from her from Kansas City. Ruth's devotion to justice for her sex had caused her to interrupt her dash westward on the "Chief." She had involved herself in a local murder trial and telegraphed:

MRS. CLAVERING MUST NOT HANG!

When Alexander Woollcott dropped dead at a microphone in 1943 after blasting Hitler, a memorial service for him was held at Columbia University. Ruth Gordon was one of the speakers. She startled several hundred listeners by her first words, "I was Alexander Woollcott's dearest friend." When she added "and so was everyone of you," she was not far wrong. Despite his cantankerousness (there were times when I thought he used rancor as a form of exercise), Alec had a talent for friendship that evidenced itself in a sometimes surprising fashion.

For example, before watching Richard Mansfield's Cyrano de Bergerac I had had another theatrical experience in my childhood that did not become clear in my mind until one evening in the 1920s when I was in New York with a group of friends whose conversation swung to their earliest childhood recollections. From a pigeonhole in my memory I dislodged a fragment that had been gathering dust since I was four or five years old:

My father and another grown-up were talking in an unfamiliar room. I was brought into their orbit when the other man said, "Come here, little boy!" and led me across the room. He pulled something away from a wall. It made a hole through which he invited me to look. I looked and I saw a group of miniature figures moving about in a bright light. They were like real people in the far distance.

Time had worn away all the attendant circumstances of the incident. A few weeks after I had recalled it to my

97

friends, Alexander Woollcott, who had been among my listeners, brought me a dinner invitation from Daniel Frohman, the older brother of Charles Frohman, the theatrical manager. It was a gay dinner party until the chatter of the half-dozen guests was halted when our host rose to his feet. For a puzzling moment he looked at me. So did the others. I was nonplused. Then with a curious gentleness he repeated the words I had heard him utter almost thirty years before: "Come here, little boy." He lifted a panel in the baseboard of a wall in his studio apartment atop the Lyceum Theater and let me look down again on actors performing a play on the stage. Alec Woollcott had quite a knack for unusual kindnesses.

Because of its latter-day employment as an adjective, the word "fun" has become almost an emetic, but fun was exactly what we had. We all shared one another's love for bright talk, contempt for banality, and dedication to the use of whatever talents we had to their best employment. If one of us commented favorably in print on another's latest work, it was because the writer had truly found merit and not merely an opportunity for logrolling. I don't mean there was constant mutual admiration. Being without psychedelic drugs or other stimuli, we had to rely on other's company for diversion. Outsiders called us the Vicious Circle.

His work on the *Stars & Stripes* led to Ross's editorial job on *The American Legion Weekly*, which he soon left to become editor of *Judge*, a comic weekly. A facet of his personality manifested itself when Ellis Parker Butler, one of America's best-known humorists, submitted something he had written for publication in *Judge*. Ross had stared at the accompanying note from Butler, which bore the letterhead ELLIS PARKER BUTLER, AUTHOR OF "PIGS IS PIGS."

"If a big man like Butler feels that drum beating is necessary, I guess I'd better climb on the bandwagon," said Ross.

For a week Ross's friends received communications from him on letterheads that were conventional except for the following quotations under his name and address:

"A splendid fellow."—*Alexander Woollcott*
"Among those present was H. Ross."—*F.P.A. in The New York World*

After *The New Yorker* was solidly established, Ross, pretending ignorance, would often listen with an imbecilically gaping mouth to something being said by a crony of which he had more knowledge than the speaker. At the conclusion of an incorrect statement he would yell with make-believe fury. "That shows you're a God-damned ignoramus!" and then proceed with lordly politeness to state the facts. However, if a comparative stranger pretentiously said something inaccurate, Ross would merely grunt an acceptant "Uh huh" and walk away.

Sometimes Ross's highly articulate ability to express editorial opinion would be oddly demonstrated. Once when he was being shown an illustration submitted for publication, he was baffled by the perspective. He looked at the picture, running his fingers through his unruly hair. (George Kaufmann once said the jungle scenes in *Chang* were shot in Ross's pompadour.)

"Do you find it confusing?" someone asked.

Ross picked up the drawing and held it at arm's length. "I certainly do," he barked. "Where the hell am *I* at?"

In the twenties Ross wore the memory of his days as a waterfront reporter in San Francisco as armor against the debilitating urbanities of New York. It was a long time before he could accept the tuxedo suit as anything but the indication of a god damned sissy or dude. When he bought his first one, anyone who told him it was becoming had to listen to a flood of invectives on New York's demoralizing pressures. He would conclude his indictment with the phrase I think he always had fun hearing himself say:

"I leave it to any fair-minded body of men!"

To celebrate the arrival in our midst of Donald Ogden Stewart and the publication of his *Mr. and Mrs. Haddock Abroad*, some of us decided to take him on a little excursion. Ross, Benchley, Mrs. Parker, F.P.A., and I elected to give him a glimpse of upper Manhattan. One afternoon, we gathered at Grand Central Station and bought tickets for 125th Street. We had group singing until the train reached its destination ten minutes later. Stewart and Mrs. Parker and F.P.A. scampered to the platform through the car's front entrance. Benchley, Ross, and I descended from the rear. Passengers waiting to board the train were a bit startled when Stewart, Dorothy, and F.P.A., watching us alight, began screaming, "Here they are, here they are!" and rushed into embraces that implied the end of years of separation.

When the group recovered from the joyful excitement of reunion, Stewart exclaimed, "And we have wonderful news for you. Dotty's pregnant!" Although the announcement was also news to her, Mrs. Parker accepted it with a modest smile and lowered head. "When is it due?" someone asked. "Any minute now," beamed the little mother. Two of us formed our arms into a seat on which Mrs. Parker placed herself for transportation to the street level. We carried her to the first of the waiting line of taxis, the driver of which was a bit nonplused as we approached. We dumped Mrs. Parker inside and closed the door. As the four of us walked away, the driver called out, "Hey, what about the lady?" "Take her straight to the delivery room," he was told. His eyes turned from us to his fare. Mrs. Parker smiled and said, "Don't start the meter. I'm feeling just fine again." She left the cab and hurried to catch up with her escorts. We spent most of our visit to Harlem in a penny arcade, where we bought souvenirs for friends at home: lucky pennies in aluminum discs and personalized pencils stamped with the names of our familiars and brief monosyllabic greetings.

John Peter Toohey seldom missed a Round Table session and, constantly price-conscious, could not resist mentioning even the occasional five- or ten-cent increases on Frank Case's modestly priced menus. When his sharp eye noted that the price of roast beef had soared from ninety cents a portion to a dollar, he called the attention of everyone to the advance. He felt the rest of us were unconcerned and needed to be tutored in thrift.

We decided John should have a gentle corrective for his overconcern. Frank Case willingly entered the plot. Going over a copy of the day's menu, we increased the cost of every item by at least 50 per cent. Frank then sent the changed price list to the printer. The next day half a dozen specially prepared menus were scattered, as usual, on the round table. In case John suspected possible misprints, a couple of them were at an unoccupied adjoining table, near John's usual seat. George Jacques, the head-waiter, and the most likable I ever knew, stood ready with another in his hand.

Watching from a distance, but keeping out of sight, we allowed John to be the first at the table. He happened to be on a cracker and milk diet at the time, and that was evidently the first item he looked at. It had soared from thirty-five cents to one dollar. His eyes opened wide as he scanned the rest of the bill of fare. Then he summoned George, who managed to keep a straight face as he confirmed every new price John pointed at.

John drummed the table, impatient to give the news to the first arrival. As I had originated the scheme, I had the privilege.

"Prepare to drop dead," said John.

"Why?" I asked absently as I glanced at the menu.

"Don't you notice something unusual?"

I lowered the menu and looked around the room. "No. Where?"

"My God," said John. "You must be blind!" He watched as Harold Ross sat down and picked up another menu. There was no reaction from Ross, who summoned George Jacques.

"George, can I have the outside slice of lamb, do you think?"

"Of course, Mr. Ross," said George, tranquilly waiting for other orders.

John leaned across the table and picked up the menus

Ross and I had apparently ignored. He thrust them back at us.

"For God's sake, read what's on them!" We were obediently studying the menus as the others joined us. They proved to be equally unobservant.

John tapped his glass for attention and announced that everything on the menu was twice what it had cost yesterday, in some cases more. "Frank Case must be out of his mind!"

I believe it was Woollcott who spoke first. "Hasn't bread and butter *always* been forty cents?"

We thought that by this time John would have realized what was going on. Not at all. He proposed that for the next four days we would all lunch at other restaurants and collect their menus for comparison. He said he would go to Delmonico's, Rector's, and other expensive places and gave us all assignments, which we accepted.

For four days John covered his route. We continued to eat at the Algonquin, growing increasingly guilty at having allowed the joke to continue.

It all ended gaily, however, when John returned, menus in hand, and was told that Frank Case had been reprimanded for his extravagant increases. John examined the new menu, which indicated Frank's remorse and contrition. Porterhouse steaks were down to twenty cents. Soups, desserts, and coffee were offered "with the compliments of the management." John caught on but quickly forgave us. He did not, however, change his ways.

One of the few persons who ever got under Frank Case's skin was Herbert Bayard Swope. Eventually, the Thanatopsis Club, which had met at various members' houses, installed itself once a week at the Algonquin in a suite Case generously put at our disposal. The card game often continued until two or three in the morning, and it was our habit to have our midnight supper sent up from the kitchen of the hotel. By this time, the poker players also included Swope, Harpo Marx, and Henry Wise Miller, Alice Duer Miller's husband. One night, without consulting others, Swope, having decided the Algonquin's food was insufficiently epicurean for his taste, ordered a lucullan spread from the Colony Restaurant. It arrived about one in the morning with an escort of Colony waiters, who brought it ostentatiously through the lobby and up to the poker game. The next day everyone but Swope ruefully exculpated himself to Frank for the aspersion on his cuisine, and Frank seemed completely mollified. However, when on the following week the Thanatopsis Club gathered as usual at the Algonquin, a printed placard on the poker table greeted us:

BASKET PARTIES WELCOME

By the late twenties and early thirties the "page opposite editorial" of the weekly editions of the *World* was filled with brilliant newspaper writing by many of the Round Table crew. Besides F.P.A.'s "Conning Tower" you would find articles by William Bolitho, Frank Sullivan, Deems Taylor, Robert Littell, and Heywood Broun. On Sundays, Ring Lardner and Robert Benchley provided hilarious copy. Most of Benchley's Sunday pieces found their way into books, but I can't recall a reprinting of Lardner's *The Diary of a Wonder Man*, which for many weeks flashed with some of his brightest humor.

For a while in the twenties Broun was the *World's* drama critic, and his reviews often glowed with puns of a quality seldom reached since Thomas Hood demonstrated that they could be dignified parts of speech. I remember one of Heywood's play reviews in which he disagreed with the author's sentimental treatment of a streetwalker.

"I am less inclined," wrote Broun, "to regard prostitutes as frail vessels wrecked by the storms of chance than as craft in the path of the trade winds."

One day I was in a group of his friends and colleagues in a crowded courtroom. We had gathered to appear as character witnesses for Heywood in a suit brought against him by an actor seeking heavy damages for Heywood's printed comment about his performance in a play. Heywood had considered it extraordinarily poor and in his review had rated it the worst acting he had ever seen. The actor was awarded one cent in damages. The following year he was a member of a cast of another play Heywood had to criticize. The next morning Heywood neatly avoided being hauled into court again. Heywood wrote:

"Mr. ———'s performance was not up to his usual standard."

Early in 1923 George Kaufman and I were invited to write the book of a musical comedy whose songs were to be written by Ira Gershwin and Harry Ruby. The only qualification made by the producer was that we call it *Helen of Troy, N.Y.* Neither George nor I thought the title very clever, but it did suggest a narrative that we thought could be funny. George was at his *Times* desk when I went to the producer's office to say we would write the show and to collect the advance. I had expected a check but instead was handed a thousand-dollar bill. As bootleggers were beginning to invest heavily in the theater, I suppose the show's backers were in that category. *Helen of Troy, N.Y.* was written quickly and after a short road trial opened in New York in the late spring.

Whenever I hear anyone assert the inevitability of jealousy among actors I think of the opening night of *Helen of Troy, N.Y.* Helen Ford, a deservedly popular young musical-comedy star, had done a fine job with the leading role, but by the time the final curtain fell, Queenie Smith, a pixie-like youngster, had won the audience completely in what had been written as a minor comedy part. The curtain calls had, of course, been predetermined. Helen, responding to shouts she knew were not for her, lifted her arms for silence and cried out, "I know who you want, and you're right. She's wonderful!" And as happy as anyone in the audience, she led Queenie from the wings, then generously rushed offstage to applaud Queenie with the rest of the cast.

In June of 1923 my mother and I sailed on the *Adriatic* for our first trip to Europe. The moment the ship passed the three-mile limit it opened its bar. No longer restricted by prohibition laws, thirsty passengers came crowding in. Within a few minutes a young man achieved distinction by his noisy, garbled talk and blurred apologies as he moved about, a highball in each hand, bumping into strangers. He reeled twice around the promenade deck before a steward escorted him to his cabin. No one knew his identity, nor did anyone except his cabin steward see him again until the ship reached Liverpool. There, pale and tottering, he was assisted down the gangplank. The cabin steward told prying busybodies that the young man had maintained a week-long jag by a supply of liquor limited by the ship's doctor to a daily quart.

When I was about to go ashore my own gabby cabin steward confided some illuminating information on the conspicuous drunk. The quart-a-day story had been false, as had been the public staggering and dipsomaniac seclusion. The young man, who had crossed the Atlantic two or three times on the *Adriatic*, had paid to have reports on his liquor consumption circulated. He was actually a very modest drinker, but he felt his business might be damaged more than his personal reputation if it became known that he was one of the owners of a widely advertised remedy for seasickness.

When we reached London my friends Fred and Adele Astaire were about to make their English debuts in *Stop Flirting*. As they were unknown to the British public, several of their American admirers attended the opening to applaud should the London audience be apathetic. It turned out to be one of the noisiest premieres on record. Overnight the Astaires became the darlings of London, and the entrancing Adele was soon surrounded by suitors. With most of England's bachelors to choose from, Adele eventually married Lord Charles Cavendish, the son of the Duke of Devonshire and brother of the Lady Anne Cavendish, one of the most brightly gay young Englishwomen I have ever met.

That year, 1923, also saw the rising star of young

Beatrice Lillie reach full brightness in André Charlot's production of *The Nine O'Clock Revue* at the Little Theatre in John Street. Her "March with Me" in which, dressed as Brittannia, she led a dozen Girl Scouts, was an unforgettable demonstration of her comic genius. It brought me to the theater night after night. A. A. Milne, whom I had met in America, was at the moment soured on all forms of theater because of the unfavorable reviews English critics had given his latest play. I thought watching Bea Lillie might be a good tonic. Acceding to his wife's persuasions and mine, he came with us to John Street. I never saw a man laugh more or be so quickly restored to cheerfulness.

Recalling Alan Milne brings to mind a delightful experience I had in 1923 at his house in Chelsea. We were having tea in the Milnes' top-floor living room. I saw Alan and his wife half-smiling at something behind the sofa on which I was sitting. In a moment two small hands were pressed over my eyes. When they were taken away I turned for my first meeting with Christopher Robin. He looked very much like Shepheard's illustrations. He was a curly-headed three-year-old with a smile that made his father happy to write about him.

Cross-Channel air travel had become a daily event by the time of my first visit to London. As I had been cursed with a fear of heights since childhood, I decided that going to Paris by plane might be therapeutic. Two airlines, the British Handley-Page and the Farman-Goliath, precursor of Air France, had daily flights scheduled between Croydon and Le Bourget.

At Croydon airport the weather was not too promising, but having reached a nadir of fear, I climbed into the world's largest airplane, the newest Handley-Paige monster. It seated eight. I had been told by experienced air travelers that boredom was the worst thing to fear while flying. Unhappily the books I had brought along to minimize ennui had somehow gone with my suitcase into the luggage compartment, and all I had to read was a brochure entitled "Travelling by Air" with photographs of and from planes thousands of feet from the ground. My preparation for the journey had included something close to a nightmare during my sleep the night before. A finger not attached to anything had pointed itself at me while a Voice of Doom assured me I would not leave England alive. After the plane left the ground and I looked through the window beside me, I was a soul liberated from hell when I saw the English Channel below. The Voice of Doom had been talking through its hat, and I felt much better.

Then, I was seized with an impulse to use my camera. Even today I feel a momentary icy wind when I remember how I had seriously begun to study the crisscrossings of wires connecting the cabin with the wings. Fear had so drained me of all normal reactions that I figured if I could get through the window by my seat I could step onto the lower wing and with a good grip on the wires take a photograph of the French coast, over which we were just passing. Fortunately, the window refused to open. I resigned myself to observing detachedly the bumpiness of the air three thousand feet above France. We made a spiral landing at Le Bourget, and I got out of the plane too numb to celebrate our safe arrival.

En route to my Paris hotel my sensory system resumed normal functioning and the flight was pushed to the back of my mind, but I carried enough psychic scar tissue to travel resolutely only on the ground until 1943, when as a writer for the War Department I had to fly. Within a few weeks I really was a seasoned air traveler, completely at ease as I boarded planes in Detroit, New Orleans, and other distant points. Sometimes flying orders led to my contentedly reading newspapers as I lolled on a pile of mail sacks in single-engined government carriers. Since the war I've never boarded a train if I've been anywhere near an airport.

My first visit to Paris had been occasioned by a rendezvous I had made a few days before sailing from New York. To the surprise of her cronies Neysa McMein had married a newcomer to the Algonquin fellowship. He was John Baragwanath, a young metallurgical engineer employed by the Guggenheims. None of us knew of the marriage until Neysa announced that she and her bridegroom had engaged passage on the White Star liner *Olympic* for a honeymoon in Europe. Less than a week before their scheduled sailing Jack told Neysa their trip would have to be postponed as the Guggenheims had ordered him to Labrador to evaluate some newly discovered mineral deposits. With his customary concern for people he loved, Woollcott, as a wedding present, had arranged for the newlyweds to find an automobile and chauffeur waiting at Biarritz to take them wherever they wished to go.

The effect of Jack's announcement on Neysa was not alleviated by his hesitant invitation to take her with him to Labrador. Neysa said she had no desire to begin her married life in an igloo. She had expected to have a summer in Europe and was boiling mad at having to give it up. She telephoned the news to Alex. Late that afternoon at a commiseration meeting in Neysa's studio, she was informed of a proposal Alec, Jascha Heifetz, and I concocted. "We three are all going to Europe," said Alec. "Why don't you sail on the 'Olympic' as you'd planned, meet us in Paris, and *we* will take you on your honeymoon?" Neysa, the girl from Muncie who rode elephants in circus parades and dashed from her studio to follow passing fire engines, agreed.

Paris in the summer of 1923 contained almost as many Americans as French. The Left Bank was swarming with the vanguard of young writers from the United States. Veterans of World War I were coming back to revisit familiar scenes. On the Rue Pigalle one heard more English than French, and such Gallic night spots as The Chicago Inn, Charley's Quick Lunch, and Bricktop's made the street cosy and homelike.

Friends of Neysa's from the Chicago Art Institute, now studying in Paris, got us tickets for the Quatres Arts Ball, which that year had the Festival of Bacchus as its theme. As they made their way in groups by foot from Montparnasse to Luna Park, the site of the ball, Parisians at terrace cafés welcomed bacchantes, fauns, dryads, and satyrs to break the journey with a drink or two. By the time the ball began, enough had been drunk to turn it into a genuine bacchanal. One of the most carefree participants was a young man who could not dance quite as lightfootedly as most of the others. He had come dressed as a Roman youth. He wore a short tunic, and a deep tan makeup covered his body. The uniform color on his legs minimized that the left was a substitute for the one he had lost as a poilu in the war.

We had engaged a compartment on the morning train to Biarritz. It left Paris very early, and we decided that, as we could sleep during the journey, our last night in Paris should be enjoyed to the utmost. With many Parisians it was a ritual after a night on the town to make a final stop at Le Café du Pére Tranquil for recuperative bowls of onion soup. It must have been about 4 A.M. when we arrived at the café. The last of its regular patrons had departed, and we climbed the stairs to the second floor restaurant to find the *patron* closing the windows against possible morning rain. Two little *poules* at a corner table were slipping into their coats and calling it a night. The violinist of the three-piece orchestra had shut his instrument case. As we entered, the musicians reconciled themselves to more work.

While we waited for our onion soup, Jascha asked the violinist if he might borrow his instrument. Jascha's first concert in Paris was still three months distant, and the violinist did not recognize him, but as he seemed reasonably sober and able to pay for damage to the fiddle, he handed it over. I have heard Jascha play many times, but never did I enjoy his genius as much as I did that morning. Everyone in the Café du Pére Tranquil quickly realized that a virtuoso was present. The departing *poules* went back to their table, cooks and waiters came from the kitchen, the orchestra listened in a state close to reverence, and with the sounds of the awakening market providing a curiously sympathetic and almost orchestral background, Jascha played Viennese waltzes until the sun came through the windows.

The honeymoon party had a fifth member when we arrived in Biarritz. He was Ferdinand Tuohey, the editor of the Paris edition of the New York *World*. We found the car Alec had originally engaged for the newlyweds waiting for us. It was a luxurious limousine that Marcel, the polished, giant chauffeur who came with it, said had been the property of the late King of Montenegro.

Marcel was an excellent driver, but we had not gone many miles before he confessed that the car was difficult to drive because of the weakness of the brakes. Despite the excellence of the Napoleonic road through the Basque Pyrénées, the chance of head-to-head collisions with tiny Citroëns that flashed past us like darning needles made me feel I knew the cause of the King of Montenegro's death.

Our progress toward Nice was leisurely. There would be halts for lunch less frequently at hotels or inns recommended in the *Guide Michelin* than in villages unrecorded on our map. When we halted in these hamlets Alec and Tuohey would forage the best local bread, cheese, sausage, and wine. Then everyone would pile back into the car, and at the first inviting spot we would have roadside meals Escoffier could not have made more delicious.

Unhampered by time schedules, we were seldom certain where we would spend the night. One afternoon was filled with unusual interest when we came to Anagra, the late Edmond Rostand's villa, where he had written several of his major plays. It was a great, rambling building on an eminence high enough to provide a panoramic sweep of the countryside. Under a great walnut tree in the garden was a wide, circular stone table, at which, the caretaker assured us, Rostand had written *L'Aiglon* and *Chanteclair*. The villa and its grounds were for sale at an absurdly low price, and for an hour we considered dashing home and trying to raise money to buy it.

It was almost nightfall when we forced ourselves to leave Anagra and seek the night's lodging. The map indicated that the nearest community with a recommended hotel was Mauléon, a half-hour's drive away. Mauléon had only a short principal street, and when we entered it we encountered a dry-land version of the mystery of the *Mary-Celeste*. There was no staff to greet us at the Hôtel de la Poste. Only silence followed poundings of the bell on the counter marked *Récéption*. Shouts at the foot of the stairway leading to the second floor brought no answer. We went out on the street on the chance that the porter or receptionist might have stepped out momentarily. The street was empty. The door of a little *épicerie* a few steps away was unlocked, but there was no one within.

We returned to the hotel. Again our calls went unanswered. Completely baffled, we made our way through the hotel's empty restaurant into a deserted kitchen. It was well stocked and as in the galley of the *Marie-Celeste*, the stove was warm from recent use. As hungry as we were puzzled, we built up the fire in the stove and cooked ourselves a satisfying meal from the ample provisions about us.

As we ate, we made conjectures, constantly hoping to be interrupted. Woollcott ventured that Mauléon had been that day visited by the bubonic plague and the inhabitants had managed to crawl away and die in a corner of the town which we could locate when we finished our coffee. Others suggested that an organized gang of *souteneurs* had raided the town shortly before our arrival, carried off every village maiden to be shipped to Rio de Janeiro's brothels, and that their relatives and friends were somewhere on the road to Marseilles, trying to overtake the kidnapers. Tuohey could only murmur that it was the God-damnedest thing *he'd* ever seen!

By the time we finished dinner it was dark. We had managed to find the electric switches that turned on the hotel's lamps, but up and down the moonlit street there was no sign of man-made illumination. We climbed the hotel's stairs and found signs of tenants in some of the rooms: clothing in closets and other personalia indicated recent occupancy. Five rooms seemed available for guests, and with a slightly eerie feeling we returned to the street floor and signed the hotel register. By 1 P.M. our speculations were not enough to keep us awake. We lugged our bags upstairs and went to bed.

I was shocked into wakefulness by a nearby explosion of sound. It was dawn, and through the window near my bed I could see it was raining heavily. Nonetheless, from immediately below my window came one of the loudest renditions of the "Marseillaise" ever heard. As I looked down I saw that this noisy barrage was coming from a dozen musicians. A few minutes later *The Case of the Town of Mauléon* was no longer a mystery. The bandsmen were blowing their heads off as a compliment to the *patron* of the hotel. He had been president of Mauléon's annual fair, which had been held half a kilometer away and enjoyed until daybreak by the entire population.

I should think that for many years the proprietor of another hotel remembered our coming to his. It was listed in the *Guide Michelin* as the choicest in Bagneres-de-Luchon. He might have been a bit surprised when four men and a woman asked for five bedrooms. If so, he underwent a greater surprise when he opened the door of the first, and his guests spied a bigger, wider bed than any they had yet beheld on their travels. Its invitation for a session of dice was too good to resist. We had enjoyed no gambling for several days, not even cribbage, casino, or backgammon, and without waiting to inspect the other bedrooms, we closed the door in his face. It was a memorable crap game. Neysa first had extraordinarily bad luck, but when it turned it did so disastrously for the rest of us. She began to make pass after pass. Finally the only sounds in the room were Neysa's loud crooning before she threw, and her triumphant yelps of delight as she made her points. Her sounds must have been audible in the hallway. When we filed out, our landlord was still there. He gasped as Neysa daintily counted the francs she had acquired, followed by four dejected cavaliers. We were evidently different from the usual run of American tourists.

At the end of July, I rejoined my mother in London, and a few days later we sailed for home. George Kaufman reported that Winthrop Ames wanted to talk with us about adapting a German play by Paul Apfel, *Hans Sonnenstossers Höllenfahrt*, which was currently a great success in Berlin. Ames was almost unique among New York producers. He was a wealthy Bostonian who directed his plays with great imagination and good taste. The year before, his brilliance had made Maeterlinck's *Bluebird* a triumph of artistry, following which his *Pierrot the Prodigal* with Marguerite Clark proved he could stage a pantomime flawlessly. I am sure his staging of *The Mikado*, *The Pirates of Penzance*, and *Iolanthe* would have won reverential respect from the crotchety W. S. Gilbert.

From a half-century of theatergoing a few moments of great achievement in play direction come readily to my mind; among them was the fanciful invention with which Ames adorned the finale of *Iolanthe* at the Booth Theater. As was traditional the curtain of the second act fell on a line of peris and peers, the Lord Chancellor and his constantly attendant trainbearer, Beefeaters, and other mortals singing a final reprise of " 'Tis Love That Makes the World Go Round" in front of Woodman Thompson's beautifully designed Parliament Square. As every voice in the cast sang out the lively strains, everyone joined hands. One little peri's feet left the ground as her burly Beefeater companions effortlessly swung her back and forth like a child on a swing. As the arc of their swing increased, one felt that if she were released she would go sailing up to the Booth's balcony, and then with no warning, we were in utter darkness, the singers and orchestra simultaneously silenced. Before the audience could begin to murmur its confusion, there was a resumption of the interrupted music. It came only from the orchestra and very softly, a whispering of strings and reeds as though from a distant point. Slowly light crept back on the stage, revealing a Parliament Square empty save for the presence of the Lord Chancellor's attendant. He stood in the middle of the stage, his eyes glued to a big telescope through which he was watching his master and all the others winging their way to fairyland.

To have a play staged by such a gifted producer-director made us read Apfel's script with eagerness. When we met with Mr. Ames we had to report that we had found Apfel's fresh technique more interesting than his plot.

"That's what I hoped you'd discover," said Mr. Ames. "How would you like to create an American story using his method of dreamlike association?"

As we talked, the germ of an idea began to stir. Within a few days George and I fashioned a rough outline for the story, a fantasy in which a young musician would go through a maze of kaleidoscopic experiences, the basic theme of which would be the ancient conflict of art and materialism. We named it *Beggar on Horseback*.

Mr. Ames hoped that we would include a passage that could be done in pantomime. We had no difficulty finding a suitable moment in the second of the two acts. It came when Roland Young, the musician, was on trial for murdering a grotesque set of in-laws, one of whom—his late father-in-law—had somehow revitalized himself and was presiding as judge. To prove that the killings were justified because of the in-laws' crassness, our hero presented a dance pantomime that his in-laws had sneered at. It was called "A Kiss in Xanadu," and Deems Taylor wrote an enchanting score for it. Mr. Ames created the wordless action in which a king and queen, bored with each other, seek romantic diversions in a moonlit park and fail to recognize each other behind masks.

Seventeen-year-old Greta Nissen, newly arrived from Oslo, was startlingly lovely as the queen, so that only a firm contract kept motion-picture companies at bay until the play completed its long run. When it closed, Greta became one of the great stars of Hollywood.

Robert Sherwood had become editor of Charles Dana Gibson's *Life*. George and I were frequent contributors along with Benchley, Dorothy Parker, and other Algonquinities. Together, George and I wrote a monthly comic almanac for a whole year. Benchley was now *Life*'s drama critic, and I'll bet there are many scrapbooks studded with his weekly summary of plays. His abhorrence of *Abie's Irish Rose* was great, and each week during its long run, his pungent comments on the play enormously stimulated *Life*'s weekly sales. Many readers went to their Bibles for enlightenment when one issue of *Life* printed the following cryptic reference to Hebrews 3:22. The researchers discovered the biblical passage "Jesus Christ, the same yesterday, and today, and forever."

Before Robert Sherwood became editor of *Life* he had been its movie critic. Not yet planning a career as a playwright, Sherwood dreamed of selling a script to the movies. Among the top directors he had met while writing criticism was Rex Ingram. Sherwood evolved an elaborate plan for interesting Ingram in a scenario he had written. It included three objectives: first, convincing Ingram that Sherwood was a man of wealth not likely to sell a movie story cheaply; second, making some headway with his courtship of a little actress named Mary Brandon; and third, providing a few friends with some lavish hospitality. The triple effort was made in the form of a dinner party in one of the private dining rooms of Delmonico's elegant restaurant on Fifth Avenue and Forty-fourth Street.

On a beautiful spring evening in 1920, Miss Brandon,

Margalo Gillmore, Dorothy Parker, Robert Benchley, our host, and I arrived in formal evening wear to help Sherwood make a good impression on Ingram and his blonde movie-star wife, Alice Terry. The dinner went haywire from the moment it began. Miss Terry, wobbly from cocktail parties she had attended during the afternoon, had decided to limit her drinking to pousse-cafés. Within five minutes Dotty Parker solicitously made the first of several trips with Miss Terry to the ladies' room. Each time they returned, Miss Terry, at Dotty's hair-of-the-dog recommendation, had another pousse café. In a moment she and Florence Nightingale Parker would withdraw, Dotty's gentle smile indicating her relish for being of service.

As the Ingrams had come directly from the last cocktail party to Delmonico's neither had changed to evening clothes. Mr. Ingram brushed away our host's inquiries about a picture he had just completed, by saying he didn't want to talk about pictures. His contract with his movie company had at last expired, thank God. He and Alice were in New York enroute to the Riviera, where he was going to paint and really enjoy life. He never wanted to see a movie again. Ingram then switched the conversation to the tweed suit he was wearing. He had just bought it. It was as fine a suit as he had ever had and had cost a fraction of what he had paid for suits in the past. He circled the table letting us examine its fine fabric. Sherwood, Benchley and I agreed on its high quality and listened attentively to its wearer's emphatic insistence that a man was crazy to pay more than thirty-five dollars for a suit of clothes.

Bob Sherwood concealed his chagrin and assured Mary we were not going to talk all night about men's clothes. Placating Mary when she felt she was not getting enough attention was a chore Bob was always patiently ready to accept. To most of us she was a bit of a trial. "Petulance," said Muriel King, the artist, "is part of Mary's lack of charm."

Mary's audible comments on her suitor's inadequacy in organizing dinner parties caused Margalo to leave the table to see what was causing the latest, protracted absence of Dotty and her patient. As Ingram's lowered head indicated he had fallen asleep, Benchley and I discreetly left Sherwood to soothe Mary and stepped through one of the dining room's French windows onto a balcony overlooking Fifth Avenue. It was still daylight. Bob and I looked down on the Fifth Avenue traffic. Conscious of the gentlemanly appearance of our black ties and dinner jackets, Bob took a patrician puff on his cigarette and remarked, "These are some of the peasant class, I presume?"

That was enough to prime the pump of gaiety. Traffic below us was moving slowly. I stepped to the balcony rail, and raising a commanding hand, shouted, "People, people!"

Benchley looked at me with only mild curiosity as pedestrians, motorists, and bus passengers all craned their necks upward. I cried out, "Your new prince!"

Without a flicker of hesitation Benchley stepped forward to the balustrade. He lifted his hands to silence unshouted cheers, then, as smoothly as though he had gone over the speech with an equerry, he assured his listeners in broken German that he did not want them as a conquered people to feel like slaves under a yoke but as chastened human beings aware that their future depended on the acceptance of a regime which they might resent but that would do its best to govern them in a kindly fashion.

Benchley promised that as soon as they evidenced self-restraint he would order curfews lifted, begin freeing political prisoners, and in time restore to qualified Americans the right to vote for local officials.

"And now," he concluded, "my prime minister and I will retire to discuss matters of state. And you have all been so cute, next Saturday night I will permit fireworks and dancing in the streets."

Many appreciative listeners below us applauded vigorously. Then as an encore Benchley and I sang several stanzas of that happy bierstubelied:

> Dreimal drei macht neine,
> Wir saufen wie die Schweine,
> Bier hier, Bier hier,
> Oder ich fall' um!

We rejoined our host and reported that the streets had been cleared and it was now safe to go home.

Helen of Troy, N.Y. had proved so successful that George and I wrote another musical comedy called *Be Yourself*. Even though it sparkled with the presence of Queenie Smith and Jack Donohue, a droll comedian regarded by Ray Bolger as America's greatest eccentric dancer, the piece ran for only a few months.

Aside from some sketches for the *Ziegfeld Follies*, *Be Yourself* was my last collaboration with George for several years. Our personal friendship continued until his death, however, and privately neither of us hesitated to call on the other for advice and help. Only a few weeks before he died in 1961 we were working together on a satirical musical play dealing with the extravagant adventures of a Jimmy Hoffa type of labor leader. Only George's waning physical strength prevented its completion.

Just before *Be Yourself* went into rehearsal, I saw an Off-Broadway performance of *The Playboy of the Western World*. Christie Mahon was played by an engaging young man named Thomas Mitchell. His Playboy was the happiest mixture of shyness and adolescent bravado I have ever seen brought to this role, and I felt he would be ideal for another dream comedy that was starting in my mind. George was apathetic about the idea, and I did not share his enthusiasm for what became his one solo effort, *The Butter and Egg Man*.

Martin Beck liked *The Wisdom Tooth*, the play I had written for Mitchell, the story of a naïve youth's struggle to retain his self-respecting individuality against the stereotyping pressures of New York's business world. Beck's eagerness to get the play into rehearsal so that it might have a profitable summer tour in Atlantic City, Asbury Park, and other flourishing beach resorts overrode my own good judgment as a playwright. The play's hasty writing was evident when it opened at the Apollo in Atlantic City. Mitchell and the others in the cast gave a weak play all the help they could, but its shaky structure needed more than good acting. It was obvious that reconstruction as well as new dialogue would be required. I felt justifiably discouraged as I watched the first-night audience flow out on the boardwalk. Someone tapped my shoulder, and George M. Cohan said he had enjoyed greatly so many good moments in the play that I was a fool to be as downcast as I seemed to be.

"All you need to do," said Cohan, "is to think the story out more clearly and you'll have a peach of a play."

Martin Beck had now joined us, and when Cohan moved away he said, "I think he's right. Let's close it for repairs."

I told him that at the moment I was bankrupt of ideas and hadn't the faintest notion of what was necessary for the play's salvation.

"O.K.," said Beck, "we'll put the sets in storage until the play's ready."

I took Beck at his word. Mitchell said he too had faith in the play and if he were not playing elsewhere, he would be glad to act in a new version. George was deeply involved in problems with *The Butter and Egg Man*, and I decided it would be best for my own troubled play if I cleared my mind of it for a while by working on something else. This resulted in my first and only production under the banner of Earl Carroll.

Carroll was an ex-theater usher who regarded himself as a genius among theatrical entrepreneurs. Restricted by a small bank account from producing plays on a grand scale, he aroused the interest of a Texas oil millionaire by advertising in the Dallas newspaper that he would be obliged to give up the theater unless some wealthy patron of the arts came to his aid. The oilman sped to New York, eager to be an angel. He was so impressed by Carroll's smoothness that he financed the construction of a handsome theater on Seventh Avenue at the edge of Times Square, and until he became bored, backed several of Carroll's productions. After the quick failure of *Baku*, an opulently mounted bit of trash written and staged by himself, Carroll decided to outdo Florenz Ziegfeld as a producer of shows featuring beautiful girls. He called several such productions *Earl Carroll's Vanities*, and his brassy imitation of the *Follies* created their own public. Carroll directed them in a beret and artist's smock that helped him sustain his role as an artist whose easel was the stage. Despite the tawdriness of his achievements he was able to persuade W. C. Fields to appear in one of his revues and to place the equally sought-after Joe Cook under a long-term contract.

Joe Cook was as versatile a comedian as America has ever produced. Orphaned as a small child, Cook had been adopted by an Indiana farmer and his wife. His foster mother certainly encouraged his enthusiasm for gymnastics.

"She thought it was fine that I wanted to be an acrobat," Joe once told me. "More than half the barn was a private gymnasium, and it had electric lights in it before they were installed in the house."

When he grew up, Cook was an incredibly versatile entertainer. He had mastered virtually every circus act calling for talent and skill. He could play almost any musical instrument, take an outstanding part in any team of acrobats, juggle a miscellany of objects from thimbles to lighted lamps, and create a kind of nonsense comedy that no one has ever successfully imitated. His monologues were so hilarious that eventually his physical virtuosity became a minor part of his repertoire. If you are not over fifty, ask almost anyone who is and learn about Cook's Rube Goldbergian machines whose complicated arrangement of pulleys, wheels, gears, gongs, and other gadgets filled a whole stage. They would operate with the help of the inimitable Dave Chasen and other stooges. The movement of their mechanical parts was accompanied by a

medley of rattles, roars, explosions, and chimes. The ultimate achievement of their operation might be the descent
of a pile driver, causing the blissfully smiling Dave Chasen
to go right through the stage.

Joe had an estate on the shore of Lake Hopatcong in
New Jersey. On weekends Ross and I would join half a
dozen or more cronies for a visit to "Sleepless Hollow."
The place teemed with unusual diversions. There was a
golf course unlike any in America. It had a single grassy
tee atop a water tower. The one green was a hundred feet
away. If your ball reached any part of it you were bound
to make a hole in one. The green being concave, the ball
would inevitably roll into a hole and pass through a pipe
to an adjacent table. When you arrived there you found
the ball and a certificate signed by your host attesting
your achievement. Elsewhere about the grounds was every
kind of circus paraphernalia, trapeze equipment, trampo-
lines, and supports for slack or tight-wire walking. All
were kept in shape for use by Joe and his two young
sons.

First visitors to Sleepless Hollow were always puzzled
by four or five small one-story structures. The assumption
that they might be guest houses was weakened by the unusually large padlocks on their doors. You never had to
wait long before their function was made known. Soon
after Ellis Rowlands, another of Joe's stooges, received you
at the door in a butler's livery, Joe would remark that his
guests were thirsty. Did Ellis know if O'Brien's speakeasy
was open? Ellis said that only today he had heard that it
was.

"Then would you phone him and say I'm bringing
some friends over?"

126

"Yes, indeedy," Ellis would reply, and disappear. Joe would improvise something about O'Brien for his guests. One time it dealt with O'Brien's remarkable ability for discovering great works of art and buying them for a fraction of their value.

"It may seem unbelievable," said Joe, "but on the walls of his saloon O'Brien has the finest collection of Rembrandts, Titians, Da Vincis, and Rubenses in the world. It's just a short walk. Shall we go?"

Joe would then lead the way to one of the small outbuildings, now unlocked, and would rap on the door. It would be cautiously opened by Ellis, in a bartender's apron. He was now Mr. O'Brien and would begin serving drinks behind a completely stocked bar. On the wall one could see only a few photographs of prize fighters and pictures from the pages of the *Police Gazette*.

"Why, Mr. O'Brien," said Joe the night we had heard of Mr. O'Brien's shrewd purchases, "you've taken down all your priceless paintings."

Ellis was usually ready for any of Joe's verbal sallies, but at the moment he needed a cue.

"Which priceless paintings did you have in mind, Mr. Cook?"

"Why your Correggios, your Giorgiones, your Tintorettos, and so on," explained Joe. "The ones that I used to admire so much on your walls. They're all gone!"

"Oh, yes," said Ellis, a bit wistful. "I know the ones you have in mind. They were all dandy, but I got tired of dusting them day after day, day after day."

"Where are they now?" asked Joe.

"I gave them to the poor," Ellis explained.

Before the night grew old, visits would be paid also to

the unpadlocked bierstube of Mr. Schultz, the bistro of Monsieur Le Grande, and the cantina of José Perez, all spitting images of Ellis. In the main house we sat down, never earlier than 1 A.M., to feasts that always included Dave Chasen's marvellous barbecued spareribs. They were so good that after Joe finally retired from the theater, Dave opened Chasen's Southern Barbecue Pit in Hollywood, which expanded into one of the country's great restaurants.

At Sleepless Hollow there would be a short introductory speech by Ellis, hard to understand because Ellis would leave dangling a long, garbled, complimentary reference to one guest and start a panegyric of another. Joe's own improvised speeches would end with his audience weak from laughter.

A handsome billiard table was about the only conventional appointment in Sleepless Hollow. Joe was very proud of a baseball resting in a glass case on a silver pedestal.

"The only one in existence," Joe informed us, "not signed by Babe Ruth."

In the same room attached to strings from the ceiling, were what Joe called the world's largest collection of objects smaller than a man's hand. If you challenged him to show a razor blade, the stub of a theater ticket, a two-cent stamp, or a referee's whistle, Joe would beam and point it out immediately. The house contained a theater completely furnished with a stage, scenery, and lighting equipment. The stage, however, was crowded when it held more than three actors. The auditorium consisted of one orchestra chair and a plush-railed box furnished with opera glasses for occupants of three comfortable armchairs. After a performance, without leaving the box, one could lean out and offer a congratulatory handshake to the artists on the stage.

The Saturday night fun seldom ended before five or six Sunday morning. If, after daybreak, someone remarked that Joe was nowhere to be found, it was truthfully explained that Joe had gone as usual to early mass.

Because of my admiration for Joe's talents I had long wanted to write a show for him. My inability to solve the rewriting problems of the play for Thomas Mitchell led to discussing a musical comedy for Joe. Joe was enthusiastic about my notion to have him play a young American multimillionaire who purchases a bankrupt Balkan kingdom, not in order to be its ruler, but so that he can return to America as its ambassador and, diplomatic privileges insured, know that his liquor would be of the highest quality. Unhappily, Joe's contract with Carroll prevented the play from being done by any other manager. Joe, who abhorred Carroll's vulgarity, obtained Carroll's promise that he would not impose himself on the staging on *How's the King?* But as he was paying for the scenery, Carroll insisted that it be made by a scenic construction company noted for its low prices and shoddy work. The first scene was the observation platform at the end of Joe's private train racing toward the kingdom he had purchased by mail. On the opening night Joe and several of the American debutantes whom he had acquired in Paris were singing the first number when the observation platform collapsed and everyone on it fell to the stage. Fortunately, no one was seriously hurt, but the incident added nothing to our respect for Mr. Carroll. This was the end of the play.

One night more than a hundred highly respected

New Yorkers attended a stag party Carroll gave after the theater's regular performance. Irvin Cobb was among those questioned by the police after Carroll was lugged off to jail for offering drinks from a bathtub containing both wine and an undraped young actress, named Joyce Hawley. Waiters distributed cups for dipping, and Carroll had hardly cried, "Drink up, gentlemen!" when raiding cops —some suspected in response to Carroll's personal invitation—arrived. Accounts of the bathtub incident were printed across the country. In Hollywood, maternal concern was stirred in the breast of a lady whose own child was famous for her striptease act. She was aghast when told that Miss Hawley had received seventy-five dollars for her stint.

"Only seventy-five dollars!" she moaned, "My God, where was her mother?"

With *How's the King?* no longer demanding attention, I was able to be objective about the revised version of *The Wisdom Tooth.* I had not promised Martin Beck any definite date for the delivery of the revisions. Less than three months had gone by since its closing in Atlantic City, but when I informed Beck that the changes had been completed, he refused to look at them. He was furious, he said, at my having written *How's the King?* He wanted nothing further to do with the play, and he now said he had no desire to be its producer. He was generous enough, however, to say that if I wanted to be responsible for its future, he would turn over all the sets and costumes for 20 per cent of any profits.

John Golden had several times asked me to bring him

a play, and he quickly booked *The Wisdom Tooth* into
the Little Theater on Forty-fourth Street, whose lease he
had bought from Winthrop Ames. Winchell Smith, himself a playwright and Golden's favorite director, took over
its staging. Smith was a highly competent man of the theater, but his broad handling of scenes that required deli-
cacy distressed Mitchell, Mary Phillips, the sensitive young
actress who played opposite him, and me. By the time we
opened in Hartford, the gentle plaintiveness we wanted to
achieve in the play's performance was missing, because of
Winchell's desire for a brisk pace. Winchell was one of
the best-liked men on Broadway. I felt I knew why when
he spoke to me after the performance.

"I've made a mistake," he said. "You understand the
play much better than I do. Why don't you take it
over?"

I had never directed a play before, but with Winchell's encouragement I became a director and for many
years staged not only my own plays but many by other
writers.

My next venture was a collaboration with another
New York Times staff member. Shortly before George
Kaufman at last resigned from the *Times*, he had taken on
an assistant named Herman J. Mankiewicz. Mank's constant
gaiety and wit made him welcome at the Round Table.
Unlike Sherwood, he was not yet concerned with writing
for the movies. Later, his *Citizen Kane* stirred both popu-
lar acclaim and the lasting wrath of William Randolph
Hearst. Mank's younger brother Joseph, then a student at
Columbia, has also made his name familiar to moviegoers.

131

Mank was eager to become a playwright, and George and I thoughtlessly agreed to collaborate with him. Mank was always ready to discuss the development of a play, but getting him to share the writing took great effort. Perhaps if he had given George and me more of his time, our resultant plays might have been better than they were. *The Wild Man of Borneo*, based on a skit I had written for Bea Lillie, and *The Good Fellow*, George's effort, survived only a few weeks' exposure. Mank was so engaging that the fun of his companionship outweighed our annoyance over his reluctance to work.

One day, at the end of lunch, Woollcott had to go to the public library for some books. Rather than go back to his desk at the *Times*, Mank volunteered to walk to the library with him. Alec left Mank for a few minutes beside the catalogue shelves and returned to find him perusing the index of authors. He pointed to the names of several of his own relatives noted for scholarly books. Earnestly, Mank said, "You may not think so, but my name's going to be in here someday, Alec."

"I believe it will too, Mank," said Alec, "if you cultivate a talent you haven't done much with so far. I can see the book now, *Herman J. Mankiewicz* by Edmund Lester Pearson." (Pearson's books about criminals were becoming very popular).

The production of *The Wisdom Tooth* brought an inquiry from Metro-Goldwyn-Mayer: Did I have any ideas adaptable for a movie story? About the same time Bea Lillie said M-G-M had invited her to appear under their banner. My suggestion that I write a picture for her resulted in my going to Hollywood and writing one called *Exit Smiling*. In it Bea played a stagestruck lady's maid. About all I remember of it was a subtitle I wish I had written but someone else did:

"She played the part of Nothing in *Much Ado About Nothing*."

Most of the stories coming out of Hollywood in those days dealt with the wild, dissipated life lived by the stars and their fantastically big earnings. Everyone knew that Mary Pickford, Douglas Fairbanks, Charlie Chaplin, Norma Talmadge, and others were being paid ten thousand dollars a week or more. My mother, who had come out to visit me, was therefore frightened when she was invited one evening to play bridge at the home of Peg Talmadge, Norma's mother. In New York my mother had become an exceptionally good bridge player and played regularly with Heywood Broun's mother and other friends. One of the funniest columns Heywood ever wrote followed some prankster's report to the police that a residential building in the East Seventies had been converted into a gambling house. That the house was the residence of Heywood's highly respected parents was not learned until a police raid scared the wits out of Mrs. Broun, my mother, and two other women who were playing bridge for a tenth of a cent a point. Heywood's column was a plea for clemency for his mother, who, he said, had led a blameless life until she'd met mine.

As never more than a dollar changed hands at the end of a wild night at the Brouns, an invitation from Norma Talmadge's mother filled mine with apprehension.

"Mary Pickford's mother is going to be there too. I've never played for a lot of money. Maybe I shouldn't go."

I said she had a reputation for skill in her own circle and urged her not to worry. "If you find the stakes too high and your luck is poor, all you need do is to leave early," I said.

Bob Benchley was in Hollywood working on a new comedy for the highly original Raymond Griffith. That night Bob and I left another party and dropped in for a midnight snack at Henry's Restaurant on Hollywood Boulevard. (Henry was a close friend of Chaplin's and played the fat man in many of Chaplin's pictures.) We were attacking hotcakes and sausages when Patsy Ruth Miller, a popular young star, joined us.

"My mother says your mother is a whale of a good card player," said Patsy.

"How does she know?"

"She just came home from a party where your mother was playing."

It was at the earliest two o'clock when I got back to my hotel. The night clerk said my mother had not yet come in. The next day she reported that the Talmadge party had not ended until nearly three.

"Then you couldn't have lost very much," I hazarded.

"Lost!" my mother exclaimed triumphantly, "I was the big winner. I won a dozen doilies and seventy-five cents in cash!"

There was another occasion that summer when my mother became socially conspicuous. Donald Ogden Stewart had become engaged to Beatrice Ames, daughter of a prominent Santa Barbara family. The wedding was to be held in a fashionable small church in Santa Barbara's suburb, Carpentaria. Don's mother had come out from Ohio for the wedding and had been living near my mother in Hollywood. Benchley was to be best man and I an usher. The day before the wedding we two drove up to Santa Barbara for a party. To make the next day's two-hour drive as comfortable as possible for Mrs. Stewart and my mother, I asked Hollywood's leading car-rental company to provide their best chauffeur-driven limousine. Because many motion-picture stars were expected as guests, all cars arriving at the church received the attention of a crowd of spectators. I was in the doorway when Mrs. Stewart and my mother alighted from a handsome Hispaño-Suiza. On alighting they were not identified by the celebrity hunters. The hearty laughter they heard as the car drove off made them look back at it. The politically conscious rental company had attached to the back of the limousine an enormous poster reading:

"Vote for Clyde Zimmer for sheriff."

That summer lingers in my memory because of another incident, in which Norma Talmadge achieved a moment of personal glory that I am sure has never been forgotten by any of her friends who were present when she earned it. Bebe Daniels and her husband, Ben Lyon, had a beach house at Santa Monica. Every afternoon scores of their friends used its dressing rooms to change from street clothes to bathing suits. Benchley and I were usually there on hot days. Late one afternoon an unusually large crowd was present. Norma Talmadge, who was then married to Joe Schenck, the head of M-G-M, had joined us. On learning that most of us had no dinner plans, she impulsively invited us to join her in the manorial

Schenck beach house next door. It was about five thirty when she dashed home to tell the Schenck butler that there would be thirty-five guests to be fed that evening. Having that many people for dinner was no strain for the Schenck household. But receiving such short notice proved to be a strain on the butler, who fortified himself for the emergency by taking more drinks than was customary with him.

About seven we all finished our drinks at the Lyon's and trooped across to the Schencks' for more. Norma greeted us and led us into a pleasant living room that would have held twice our number. I can still see the slow, dignified pace of the butler as he approached with a great silver tray holding nearly forty cocktails. His slow walk prevented the glasses from spilling more than a fraction of their content.

One of the most April-like ingénues in Hollywood was a wisp of a girl named Pauline Starke. In lowering the tray to where she was seated, dressed like a doll in a dainty long dress, the butler did a complete job of it. A cascade of cocktails drenched Miss Starke. With broken glasses at his feet and the empty tray dangling at his side and a sodden Miss Starke being tended to by an onrush of guests, the butler was the most contritely sad man I had ever seen. The nervous, hysterical laughter about him did not lessen his wretchedness. It was then that Norma Talmadge rose to the occasion. She crossed to the butler like a compassionate nurse, put her arm around his shoulder, and as she walked with him from the room sympathetically made the remark that surely is put to her credit in Heaven:

"You know, Charles, someday you and I must go on the wagon."

Going to Europe had become an annual habit. The influx of tourists increased annually up to the panic year of 1929. Paris was the focal point for every advantaged traveler. The city was truly gay, inexpensive, and beautiful. The boulevard theaters were open well into the summer. I knew a score of French playwrights and saw most of their plays. I usually stayed at the little Hotel San Regis near the Rond Point on the Rue Jean Goujon. I've always admired the French habit of naming thoroughfares after distinguished artists. Jean Giraudoux had not been dead a year when a mile-long street in Paris became the Rue Jean Giraudoux. It is good to know that a short American street in New London, Connecticut, now bears the name of Eugene O'Neill. But how many other thoroughfares here have been renamed for writers?

The Rond Point area on the north side of the Champs Élysées held constant fascination for me because every afternoon it was crowded with children. For the smaller ones, there were two puppet theaters on the Rue Mariquay corner, and a *gaufretterie* so popular that every other child's face was powdered with the sugar from its waffles. On the Champs Élysées side customers were always in line to ride the carrousels. Each was operated by hand by a weary man while the plump and usually mustached *madame caisse* collected the few sous from each patron. When school was dismissed early on Thursday afternoons a small army of stamp collectors would flock to the Bourse de Timbres. As many as twenty dealers sat at the folding tables surrounded by juvenile, pint-sized clientele.

The owners of the two puppet theaters were jealous competitors. The day the word spread among the nursery set that the villain in the cast of the Théâtre Anatole was going to appear in a new costume, every foot-high seat at its matinee was occupied. Squeals of "regardez les vêtements" were as loud as the everyday cries of delight or reproval at the action on the miniature stage. After a few minutes of infantile bedlam at the Anatole, I strolled the short distance to where le patron of Le Vrai Guignolet was glaring in the direction of his rival's place of business.

"He is a *salaud individu,* that one," said the owner of Le Vrai Guignolet. "He knew that next week I am putting new costumes on half of my characters. It is so typical of him and of others in his family. They are a low breed who can do nothing original. Also, they are trespassers and squatters with their Théâtre Anatole. Le Vrai Guignolet has been on this spot since 1784. Rather than letting decent people alone they have tried every kind of shabbiness to copy us."

"When did the Théâtre Anatole come here?" I asked.

"Not until 1816," snorted the outraged victim of johnnies-come-lately.

On Neysa's honeymoon trip I had seen the French Riviera for the first time. I made a second visit the summer of 1925 when Philip Barry invited me to spend a fortnight with him, Ellen, his wife, and their two small sons at their Villa Lorenzo in Cannes, named for Ellen's brother, Lorenzo Semple. Phil said a friend of his, also a writer, would drive down with us. During our two-day journey from Paris, the three of us talked of theater and books unceasingly. All of us were looking for titles for works in progress. My new acquaintance offered a generality about titles that I still think curiously true. He said all that is really important in a good title is that it have bones.

This writer, too, was an American, in Europe on a Rockefeller grant. He had written a play with John Farrar, the editor of *The Saturday Review of Literature*. I remembered seeing it. It was called *The Awful Mrs. Eaton*, and its big scene, purportedly of a Presidential reception in the White House, had also been made grotesque by the aforementioned octagonal library set from William A. Brady's hoard of veteran scenery.

"What are you working on now?" I asked him.

"I've just started a long narrative poem about the Civil War. I hope to finish it before I go back."

"Will you have to do much research?"

"Yes, but I think I can get all the stuff I need from the American Library in Paris."

The name he was going to give it seemed to Phil and me a good one. It was to be called *John Brown's Body*.

Stephen Vincent Benét was one of the many authors renowned in other areas who labored without much success in the theater.

In the twenties, Dorothy Parker collaborated with Elmer Rice on *Close Harmony*, which Arthur Hopkins produced. Shortly after the play closed, a group of us were discussing the methods of contemporary stage directors. Someone spoke of the nose-to-nose school of George M. Cohan. Facing his actors closely as they were deaf was one of Cohan's mannerisms. There was mention of the rather pompous Augustus Thomas, who would sit in out front and speak to actors on the stage through a megaphone.

"No, no, dear Miss Rambeau," he would say sententiously, "I like the extended arm, but keep the palm of your hand up, otherwise the speech will be negative."

Philip Moeller's delicate nuances were cited. When Arthur Hopkins' name came up, Dotty Parker remembered that when directing *Close Harmony* he had rarely, if ever, interrupted rehearsals with comments. It was his belief that if the actors thoroughly understood the play it was best to let them work out their own readings and business. Dottie thoughtfully observed:

"And there's the Arthur Hopkins honor system."

Somerset Maugham, Graham Greene, and Thornton Wilder have been among the few novelists who were at home in the theater. Henry James burned with a hunger to write for it. In England his literary prestige was great enough to make London managers overlook his theatrical failures until seven farces convinced them of his limitations. That some of his stories had dramatic potential, however, has since been proved by contemporary dramatists.

Several talented American playwrights made themselves well known in the twenties. O'Neill will presumably be the longest remembered. From Philadelphia came the facile and very witty George Kelly, whose niece Grace is not unknown. George's comedy *The Showoff*, the outstanding play of 1924, would have held that position in many other theatrical seasons. (The first of many loud protests against the selection of Pulitzer Prize-winners rose when the Pulitzer committee, which included several members of the Columbia University faculty, honored Hatcher Hughes, a Columbia teacher, for his *In Abraham's Bosom*, a greatly inferior contender. A few years later Kelly's admirers were only slightly mollified when his *Craig's Wife* was given the Pulitzer award.) The following year he wrote *The Torchbearers*, that classic revelation of the hilarities of amateur theater. On the opening night of *The Torchbearers*, George, by nature a shy man, appeared on the stage after repeated cries of "Author!" His quiet remarks to the audience were interrupted from the gallery by cries of "Louder!" Without hesitance George said:

"It isn't important," and quickly ended his speech.

George Bernard Shaw delivered another memorable curtain speech one night when he appeared in response to clamorous applause from the stalls. A heckler in the gallery yelled:

"It's a stinker!"

Shaw smiled up at his critic.

"I know it is," he said, "but who are you and I among so many?"

Many evenings during that summer in Paris, Hope Williams, the actress, and Grace Hendricks, who had an apartment at No. 1, Rue Git le Coeur, and I would cross the Pont Michel and dine at the Auberg de Vert Galant on the Île de la Cité. The *patron* welcomed our business but barely tolerated the singing to which we were addicted. When Grace carried the air of "Kentucky Babe," Hope made chords with her contralto triads and I supplied tenor bell effects. We enjoyed our harmonies greatly. We had almost finished dinner when the proprietor was awed by seeing Chaliapin and Morris Gest approach our table. He was a bit taken aback when Gest complimented our choral work and hoped we would make the trio a quartet by engaging the services of the client he had brought with him. With gravity we looked at Chaliapin as though we had never seen him and asked if he had had vocal experience. With the eagerness of an applicant for a job in an opera chorus, Chaliapin said he was a practiced singer and hoped we could use him. After an exchange of conferential looks, we regretfully informed him that as we were so accustomed to working as a trio it would be too hazardous to take on an additional voice.

"What do you sing?" Hope asked.

"Bass baritone," said Chaliapin, "I am very good."

"I don't say you aren't," conceded Hope with cool finality. "Go get a little more practice and come around next year."

Resignedly the applicant and his agent went back to their own table. *Le patron*'s face was something to see.

The Rue Pigalle was usually crowded until early mornings. *Boîtes de nuit*, like Le Rat Mort, Le Jardin de Ma Soeur, and American institutions like Bricktop's and Mitchell's Chicago Lunch were always filled with refugees from Prohibition. One of them, Sigourney Thayer, had decided not to let a temporary money shortage deprive him of a summer escape to Europe. A day after the *Aquitania* had dropped its pilot at Ambrose Light, a puzzling error in cabin assignments was discovered by the chief purser. A passenger who obviously should have been traveling first class had been discovered in a steerage cabin. The purser went below to investigate. He found Sigourney placidly sitting on the edge of a bunk, quite prepared to share a room with five other passengers. Sigourney wore formal morning dress—striped trousers, cutaway coat, and ascot tie and was carelessly holding gray gloves and a silk hat. He said he was ready to make the best of the crowded quarters, having discovered that he had been fleeced by a secretary who had left his employment the previous day. Sigourney had not looked at the steamship ticket the secretary had handed him, assuming that it was an upper-deck stateroom. It was obvious now that the fellow had pocketed most of the money given him for its purchase. Sigourney said he had attended a friend's wedding at high noon and had not discovered until he boarded the ship that his wallet contained only a few dollars instead of the several thousand in drafts and bank notes he had placed in it. The purser explained that no one on the ship could sell passage, but Sigourney and his elegant luggage were moved into a first-class stateroom.

Early one morning a few days later Sigourney was challenged by some exhilarated companions on the Place Pigalle to budge single-handedly a huge drum of telephone cable standing in the street. Sigourney put his shoulder to the drum and discovered it had not been wedged. It began to roll with increasing momentum toward the Rue Pigalle. Shouts of warning caused some quick scampering as the drum started down the steep street with increasing speed. By a miracle, when it finally swerved into a building almost at the foot of the hill, no one had been hurt. Sigourney discreetly retired before the gendarmerie arrived.

(5)

The Green Pastures

IN NEW YORK, in the fall of 1928 I encountered my friend
Rollin Kirby, owner of a portfolio of Pulitzer Prize
citations for his cartoons in the New York *World*.

"I've just read a book you'll like," said Rollin.

On his advice I bought a copy of *Ol' Man Adam an'
His Chillun* by a writer named Roark Bradford. I read it
that night and the following day telephoned Richard
Walsh, one of the editors of Harper's, who had published
it. Bradford, he said, was a young journalist living in New
Orleans and who might be interested in my basing a play
on his work. I had found a book filled with a new and delightful way of retelling some of the stories of the Old
Testament.

Bradford, born in Tennessee and from infancy familiar with the Negro field hands on his father's plantation,
was by nature a deeply compassionate man. He understood the spiritual starvation of the slave and his acceptance of some of the fundamentals of the white man's
Bible. The five Books of Moses come to life for the invariably illiterate slaves when early black preachers, ordained
only by their personal faith and popularity as speakers,
placed the biblical occurrences in familiar neighborhoods.
In *Ol' Man Adam an' His Chillun* Bradford had used
Louisiana as the general background for his own recounting. Cain, after interrupting his plowing of the south forty

to kill Abel, fled to Nod Parish, where he married a local girl whose home might have been close to Baton Rouge. The Prodigal Son came back to the farm after a spree in New Orleans.

I think the idea of using the rich folklore Bradford had invented came when I saw the illustrations that were in my copy of the first edition. There were frequent line drawings of God. Bradford had been less interested in God than in his poignant, absurd and noble, creatures here on earth. He had accepted the illustrator's depiction of God as a stereotype southern planter with black fedora hat, goatee, and cane. I did not immediately see what was to become the backbone of the play, but that God, a fundamentalist God, should be a dominating character was in my mind from the beginning.

Within a few days after my first talk with Dick Walsh, I had signed the contract for the dramatic rights to *Ol' Man Adam an' His Chillun*. It was understood that my intention was not simply to string together and present in theatrical form what Bradford had written as a collection of individual sketches. I wanted to use them and their manner of telling in a play that would have its own dimensions. I planned to write what would be essentially a religious drama for which the sketches would be a loose framework.

Although I did not yet have an architectural blueprint of the play's structure, I wrote what I felt might be an important scene. It dealt with Goliath's destruction by little David and later proved troublesome. I have included it later in this story.

Writing dialogue has always been comparatively easy for me at the final part of my plays' construction. I have heard of playwrights who can start writing dialogue the moment the play begins to take shape in their imagination, but I've always been dubious about such claims. If there's a copy of "Kubla Khan" that Coleridge jotted down the moment he woke up from that dream, I'd like to see it. George Kaufman and I never tackled our work in that fashion, and every time I've written a play alone I've followed what to me is the only practicable method. I don't offer it as an infallible procedure, but it's the only one that works for me. Ideas for plays come from everywhere: meeting or reading about an unusual individual; some experience the writer may have had; an item in a newspaper; an exciting point in philosophic contemplation; a sudden concern with the possibilities of a new (to the writer) technique; or a detached, isolated incident, remembered or imagined.

If the germ begins to take shape, I consider it as I would an unknown but highly attractive woman. If the playwright can restrain himself from plunging into a whirlwind love affair, as if with a woman he doesn't know well, the results of his relationship may be happy. There is no need for him to repress his love. He should be constantly attentive and learn everything he can. His ardor can grow with all sorts of engaging fancies, but if he is serious, the moment comes when, just as he would want a proper residence for a bride-to-be, he must provide a dwelling for the play's idea. This demands objectivity, a sort of dual personality: the schizophrenic playwright must turn into an architect-builder.

I am a slow worker in the masonry and carpentry departments, and I knew the dramaturgy might take considerable time. I also knew that my bank account was running low. I had never met Otto Kahn, the Maecenas of the theater. I telephoned him. He invited me to his office the next day to discuss whatever was on my mind at lunch. When we finished eating he gave me a check for the five thousand dollars I had asked him to lend me. He was unwilling to accept interest but accepted my pledging of that amount against my life insurance.

My mother and I were then living in the old Rembrandt Apartments on Fifty-seventh Street next to Carnegie Hall, reputedly New York's first duplex apartment house. From its beginning it had been a warren of writers, painters, and musicians. My own apartment on the fifth floor had been tenanted exclusively by playwrights. Clyde Fitch had occupied it first. When he died, George Broadhurst moved in, and I acquired it when Broadhurst moved to a place he had built in Connecticut. For two months I wrestled with the problems of what I knew would be a play of many scenes and moments of pageantry. As their sequence began to form, I realized slowly but with increasing clarity what it was I was trying to accomplish. It wasn't until I had the dramatic blueprint clearly before my mind's eye that I saw that my narrative would concern man's ancient, intensive search for his own soul.

The Western theater begins with the satyr plays of the pre-Athenic Greeks. The altar was part of the setting for the vernal theatricals that invoked the favor of the deity. The Bacchic festivals also were attempts by God's creatures to relate themselves to Him. It seemed to me that in embracing Christianity the slave was making a similar attempt to find divinity within himself.

I had found rich promise in the vision of Negroes

uprooted from their African culture, ties broken with animistic theology, looking with hope and reverence to Jehovah and Christ. My play, then, would try to interpret a spiritual phase of the Old Testament. The search of God for man, and man's search for God. With this much of the play clear in my mind, I laid down a few ground rules. The most important was to eschew all temptations to be funny for fun's sake. Just as every moment of comedy Bradford had written was bright with the southern Negro field hand's innocence, I must guard against the imposition of any humorous concept not racially proper.

I am not a religionist. To me, any creed that has lasted more than five hundred years has merit in it somewhere, but I have never been able to accept insistences by hierarchies or sectarian policing. As an agnostic, I recognized that I must at all times respect the faith of the black fundamentalists.

Roark Bradford lived in New Orleans. I decided I should tell him about the black, anthropomorphic, paternal God I intended to present, moving through a good stretch of Old Testament time. With the play's skeleton fairly well articulated, and with the play's beginning, the expository Sunday school scene, written, I bought passage on the S.S. *Dixie,* which carried passengers and freight between New York and New Orleans. I planned eight writing periods each day during the voyage. We had fair weather through the whole voyage. I would get up at eight and by nine be at the typewriter in my cabin. Each hour I would write dialogue and business for forty-five minutes, and then go on deck for fifteen. When the *Dixie* swung around the Florida keys into the Gulf of Mexico, I had more than half of the first of the play's two parts written. When we docked at New Orleans the first draft of the play's first half was virtually completed.

My meeting with Roark Bradford confirmed the implications of his book. Warmth and an affection as deep as his sympathy for the Negroes' social and economic plight manifested themselves in our first few minutes together. We were good friends before the day was over, and stayed so until Brad died in 1948. Mrs. Bradford was an incurable invalid, a gentle, lovable woman who smilingly reflected Brad's love and solicitude. On my first trip to New Orleans the Bradfords were living in one of the old houses with iron-grilled balconies on Jackson Square, while their permanent home, an even older house at 719 Toulouse Street in the Vieux Carré, was undergoing repairs.

I was delighted when Brad said he liked what I had written and felt confident that the second part of the play would not let the interest down.

I planned to hold the play together by having Negro melodies sung during the many scene changes, and Brad helped me select them. The social status of the Louisiana Negro today may be better than it was then. It could hardly be worse. Brad knew many Negro musicians, and for several nights they came to the Bradford house. Because of their friendship for Brad and their fear of causing him trouble in the community, one or two would invariably arrive through the back door, despite Brad's insistence that they use the front entrance like any other welcome guests.

There are two outstanding canons of conduct in the fundamentalist Negro churches, indicating differences as definite as the deep-water and the sprinkling forms of baptism. Some churches permitted social dancing, others did not. The latter tolerated and even encouraged what was euphemistically called "walking." The jump-ups, the simple airs that could be shouted as well as sung, permitted a joyful outlet for physical energy much more exhausting than the other sect's dancing. Edna-Mae Hubbard, the pianist, had a large repertoire of spirituals and "jump-ups" sung in Negro churches. "Rise, Shine and Give God the Glory" which the angelic choir sings at the fish fry is a typical "jump-up." It and almost all the rest of the music in the play came from those evenings on Jackson Square.

Clergymen in the New Orleans area could be racially identified by a method that allowed editors to list Negro churches and white churches together in their religious columns but gave subtle notice to churchgoers from out of town. If, in the listings of churches, the presiding minister had the words "The Reverend" before his name, the reader knew he was white. If he was termed "Reverend" he was, of course, black.

The presence of whites in Negro churches was rare, but Brad managed to take me to several where we were welcomed. I talked with a dozen Mr. Deshees. Like my Sunday school teacher they were illiterate but could quote long passages from the Bible, seeming to be reading words that were actually meaningless to them. Index fingers moving along the lines of the printed page made their innocent pretense seem authentic.

I felt I should know something about the Negro "barrelhouse" dives before writing the Babylon scene. I was staying at the Hotel Roosevelt in New Orleans, following a schedule that had me working most of the mornings and afternoons and going to bed around 8 P.M. Shortly before two in the morning I would get up and

Marcus Carlon Cook, my grandfather

Left: Mother, in pose for pho-
tographer-son

Below: Hotel White, McKeesport, Pa.

M.C. as a six-year-old thespian

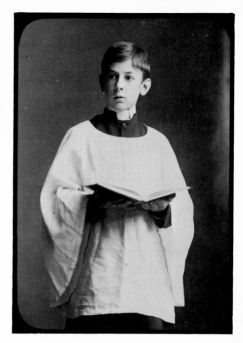

Pride of the choir

Early calligraphy (age 11)

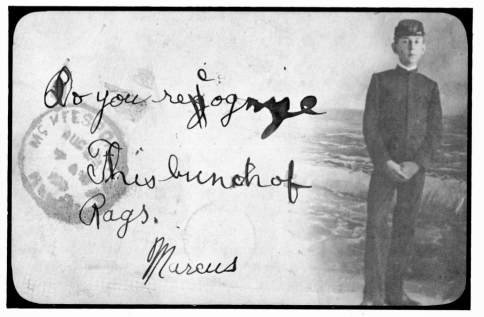

Depression gaieties (L to R), Phillip Loeb, Jack Haley, Charles Winninger, Charles Butterworth, Hugh O'Connel and M.C.

At Sea at Coney Island (L to R), Constance Collier, Noel Coward, Harold Ross, M.C. and Jed Harris

Cruisers in Stockholm, 1933 (L to R), M.C., Arthur Samuels, unidentified gentleman, Edna Ferber, Madeline Connelly, Pearl Buck, Allison Smith, Russel Crouse, Vivian Martin, two unidentified ladies, Julia Ferber and Louis Bromfield

Connelly Patio in Hollywood, 1935 (L to R), Mrs. Ernest Pascal, William Faulkner, his Agent, Ben Wasson, Dorothy Faulkner

Left top: Russel Crouse and Friend in Norway, 1933

Left middle: Studied Insult for Harold Ross in Lapland

Left bottom: F. P. A. enjoying the Caribbean

Right: Neysa McMein and her honeymoon escorts (L to R), Alexander Woollcott, Jascha Heifetz and M.C.

Below: Robert Benchley and M.C. finding something funny

Dorothy Parker in oil by Neysa McMein

Bob Sherwood's wedding party. Among those present, Top Row (L to R): The Groom, Benchley, Sidney Howard, unidentified gentleman, Frank Case, the Bride's father, unidentified gentleman, Alec Woollcott, Grant Mitchell, John Emerson; Middle Row (L to R): The Bride (Mary Brandon), unidentified lady, two unidentified gentlemen, Margalo Gillmore, M.C., Douglas Fairbanks; Bottom Row: two children.

KUNGL. DRAMATISKA TEATERN

Måndagen den 14 November 1932 kl. **8** e. m. (precis)

För 30:de gången:

Guds Gröna Ängar

(The Green Pastures)

Biblisk legend i 2 avdelningar (19 bilder) av **MARC CONNELLY**.

Översättning av *J. N. Reuter*, Dekorationerna av *Sven-Erik Skawonius* och *Olov Molander*, Musiken arrangerad efter andliga negersånger av *Sune W. Engström* och *Björn Schildknecht*. Sångerna utföras av *Wiggers-kvartetten* med ackompanjerande kör. Dansen av *Sven Tropp.*

Regi: *Olov Molander.*

Personerna:

Herren Gud .... Georg Blickingberg

Mr. Deshee, en gammal negerpräst	Carl Browallius	Sem	Kotti Chave
Första köksan	Sally Palmblad	Ham	Gunnar Sjöberg
Andra köksan	Frida Winnerstrand	Jafet	Axel Janse
En fet ängel..................................	Tyra Dörum	Isak	Ivan Hedqvist
En mager ängel	Renée Björling	Moses	Gabriel Alw
Gabriel	Carl Barcklind	Sippora, hans hustru.................	Signe Enwall
Adam-Hezdrel	Edvin Adolphson	Aron	Gösta Hillberg
Eva	Wanda Rothgardt	Farao	Sven Bergvall
Kain	Semmy Friedmann	Övermagikern	Josua Bengtson
Kains flicka	Karin Ekelund	Josua	Bror Bügler
Zeba	Märta Ekström	En spejare	Folke Hamrin
Kain den sjätte	Håkan Westergren	Kungen av Babylon	Olof Winnerstrand
Noak	Torsten Winge	En profet	Gunnar Sjöberg
Noaks hustru	Ellen Borlander	Översteprästen	Axel Högel
		Skolbarn, änglar, städerskor, hovfolk hos Farao, Josuas stridsfolk, cabaretgäster i Babylon, Hezdrels krigare.	

Första avdelningen.

Bild 1. **Söndagsskolan.**	Bild 7. **Guds kontor.**
Bild 2. **Guds gröna ängar.**	Bild 8. **Herren Gud vandrar på jorden.**
Bild 3. **Paradiset.**	Bild 9. **Noaks hem.**
Bild 4. **Söndagsskolan.**	Bild 10. **Arken bygges.**
Bild 5. **Brodermordet.**	Bild 11. **Arken på havet.**
Bild 6. **Kains flykt.**	

Andra avdelningen.

Bild 12. **Guds kontor.**	Bild 16. **Babylon.**
Bild 13. **Den brinnande busken.**	Bild 17. **Guds kontor.**
Bild 14. **Faraos tronsal.**	Bild 18. **Jerusalem.**
Bild 15. **Tåget genom öknen.**	Bild 19. **Guds gröna ängar.**

Ett längre uppehåll mellan de båda avdelningarna.

Kl. **8** (precis)—omkr. 11 e. m.

Tisdagen:

Guds gröna ängar.

Veckorepertoar: Onsdag, Torsdag: **Guds gröna ängar.** Fredag: **Föreställning för Skådebanan.** Lördag: **Guds gröna ängar.**

The Green Pastures program at the Royal Theater in Stockholm

Gabriel and small fry

Richard B. Harrison and Alonso Fenderson (God and Moses)　　　　Right: Exodu

Unretouched. Used by Theater Arts. May be ordered from now.

 # 27

Left: Mr. Harrison

Below: M.C. with Eddie Anderson as Noah

Right top: Heaven in Hollywood

Right bottom: Actors and Director

Top: Three small Daisies

Author in 1965 defending himself against Patrick Sutton

dress and wait for the phone to ring. When the night clerk advised me that callers were waiting for me in the lobby, I would go down and join two members of the New Orleans detective force. The first time it occurred, the clerk must have wondered what occasioned their appearance. That they didn't demand the number of my room and break in unannounced must have lessened his fears somewhat. He saw me come down and leave the hotel without the employment of handcuffs. Three hours later he saw me reappear, released from custody. On the fourth night, I was touched by the aching curiosity in his eyes as he handed me my key. I felt I should give him a hint of the reason for my presence.

"We've about finished our work," I said. "We had to hunt for parts of the body all over town, but now we know who she was and where her husband went with the money. Being an ex-President won't help him. Good night."

It would have been less interesting to have told him that under official guidance I had been observing Negro night life. None of the places we visited came alive before midnight. In several of them my escorts were recognized, but they were welcomed as old friends. Some customers even chuckled with an absence of ill-feeling as some of their proclivities were revealed to me.

"Lily, here, is one of the best panel girls in town, aren't you, Lily?"

A panel girl, I was told, assists a friend conversing in bed with a client by slipping through a panel in the wall and going through the man's pockets.

Lily laughed at the friendly reminder. "It's so if you say so," she rejoined gaily.

At Brad's suggestion a young lawyer took me on a

visit to a crumbling manor house not many miles from
Baton Rouge. The Big House, still evidencing the elegance
of a vanished era, was built in the late eighteen-thirties.
Almost a century later it was the home of three gently
bred old ladies, the daughters of the owner. A weather-
beaten card attached to a sagging wrought-iron gate read:

ROSEDAWN
Admission: 25 cents
Please pay superintendent.

Our car followed a once impressive driveway past life-size
Roman statues lining the winding road.

Getting me to see Rosedawn was only one reason for
the trip. Another one was to discover, more by surmise
than any direct statement from the Bowman ladies, the circumstances under which they were living. Besides being
their lawyer, Brad was also their unofficial guardian.
Sometimes on his quarterly visits he discovered that the
servants had not been paid since his last appearance and
might not have disclosed the fact if food had not been
running low. He would then quietly sell a couple of hundred acres of turpentine trees, pay backwages, and assure
the old ladies their finances were in modest but healthy
condition. We were received in a drawing room by Miss
Sally Bowman, ninety-one, the eldest of the sisters and the
plantation's chatelaine. In balancing my cup of tea I almost
knocked over a firescreen "sweet Mrs. Custis Washington" had given to Aunt Deborah. Audubon had stayed at
the plantation while pursuing his ornithological researches
in the South. There were several family portraits he had
painted while a guest. We were shown a dining room
where at meal times Miss Sally sat at the head of the long

table, a thin silver whistle at her side with which to summon the butler. On the paneled walls hung a dozen Sully portraits whose sale would have ended forever the sisters' need for money. If the air was sultry, Miss Sally nodded to the small Negro boy in a corner, who would pull the cord that moved the blade of a punkah fan above the table.

My interest in the original wallpaper brought me an invitation to see that in the rooms on the second floor. It had all been brought from France when the house was new. Opening a door at the end of a hall, I found a room filled almost to the ceiling with objects swathed in burlap. I was told the chamber was known as "the furniture room." The covered objects, Miss Sally informed me, were tables, chairs, and other pieces Papa had imported from England, intending them as a gift to the White House when his friend, Henry Clay, assumed the Presidency. "Unfortunately," Miss Sally concluded, "Mr. Clay did not become President, and we have just never got around to using the furniture ourselves."

At Rosedawn and one or two other places, I tested the Negro dialogue I had written, mindful of Robert Burns's habit of reading his poems in dialect to peasants for criticisms of their authenticity. A country innkeeper's daughter is said to have been unimpressed when she listened to "The Cotter's Saturday Night," remarking that she found it not at all poetical, merely an example of the way people talked.

What I read to field hands provoked some heartening, favorable reactions, but I decided I should make a more thorough inquiry. When the playscript was completed I made a second trip South and talked with a score of unlettered citizens. If a word or phrase was strange to my listeners, I rewrote it. I also acquired colloquialisms that seemed worthy of incorporation.

The writing was completed in New York. The six bound copies of the script I got from the typing bureau were soon in the hands of managers who had indicated an interest in reading any play I might write. Dotty Parker, who had generously transcribed the Exodus scene for me, said she had cried while typing it, and I felt reasonably proud of what I had produced.

I had never used an agent and began to feel the play might need a very good one when the tendered manuscripts came back accompanied by notes not at all heartening. Crosby Gaige said he had got a lot of laughs out of it but couldn't say he liked it. Philip Moeller, reading it for the Theater Guild, found it outrageously sacrilegious. Others were almost equally offended. Arthur Hopkins was the only one of the first recipients to offer a word of encouragement.

"I liked it," he told me over the telephone, "and I've read it twice. If I knew how it could be produced, I think I'd do it." Three weeks later I had been assured by every producer I had approached that *The Green Pastures* was not anything they'd want. Most friends who read it gave me encouragement. Some liked it enormously. My friend Robert Edmond Jones, who had designed many of Arthur Hopkins' fine productions, was unhappy to learn that Hopkins had turned it down. As the months rolled by, the nearest it came to production were half a dozen discussions with Jed Harris. Harris had a wonderful editorial mind, and his direction of *Broadway*, *Coquette*, and other productions sparkled with his inventive imagination. In the thirties he helped Thornton Wilder turn a structurally weak script into a masterpiece. Unhappily, he was also a martinet, and stories of his backstage battles were constant news items.

He could also be one of the gayest companions. Until 1946, when I went with him to London to be in his production of *Our Town*, I spent many happy days with him. Unfortunately, we could not agree on the production method for *The Green Pastures*, and I had to decline the contract he offered me.

With no one in sight willing to produce the play, I reconciled myself to the belief that if the play had theatrical merit, someday someone might recognize it. My bank account during the summer of 1929 received stimulus through a commission from RKO to write and appear in six two-reel movie comedies. Talkies had come in, and Richard Currier, the producer-director with RKO, had seen me act in several of the annual Dutch Treat Club shows George and I had collaborated on, and others I did alone. Two or three of those, written for the amusement of the Dutch Treat Club membership, had subsequently been given public displays. They were printed in *The New Yorker* and sold to Dwight Deere Wiman as skits in his series of Little Shows.

In June and July we completed four of the shorts, but use of the studio for other productions postponed filming the last two until October. The interval allowed me to enjoy one of the happiest experiences of my life.

Over the years I had frequently been the guest of John and Alice Garrett in their Baltimore home. John was a grandson of one of the founders of the Baltimore & Ohio Railroad. The hospitality of their baronial residence had enabled me to form many new friendships. It was there I first met Walter Damrosch. The interests of the Garrett guests varied greatly. One would find actors and musicians, poets and painters; Ignacia Zuloaga did two pictures of Alice there; and ranking government officials were almost always present. At the end of a night's gaiety, Nicholas Longworth, Speaker of the House of Representatives and husband of Alice Roosevelt, would keep the party going another hour by playing piano duets with Dr. Damrosch.

It was there I also met the fabulous Dr. Hugh Young. During World War I, Hugh had been Surgeon–General. He had performed prostate operations on Clemenceau and other European statesmen, had discovered mercurochrome, and given a new stomach to Diamond Jim Brady. Brady's years of gormandizing had laid him low when he was brought to Johns Hopkins for Hugh's attention. Hugh's repairs to Brady's interior were successful and helped give Brady six more years of life. Convalescent, Brady asked Hugh to name his fee.

"You are a wealthy man," said Hugh, "and as whatever I receive from you I intend to give to Johns Hopkins, I shall not name an arbitrary fee. Give me what you feel is proper." Brady was indeed wealthy and also grateful. The millions which created the Brady Urological Institute were his response.

Because no producer of *The Green Pastures* was in the offing, I eagerly embraced the Garretts' invitations to join them on a month's cruise of the eastern Mediterranean at the beginnning of September. John had chartered Anthony Drexel's *Sayonara*, then one of the world's largest and most luxurious yachts for a four weeks' cruise. Its crew numbered more than sixty.

Hugh Young, Helen Woods, the niece of John Pierpont Morgan and wife of former New York Police Commissioner Arthur Woods, Mary Rogers, who had just divorced H. H. Rogers, the oil magnate, and I boarded the *Sayonara* with our hosts at Genoa. The course of our progress had been determined to follow more or less the route of Odysseus. We dropped anchor at Naples to take on board two old friends of the Garretts', Sir Rennell and Lady Rodd, who had been waiting for our arrival at their summer place in Posillipo. Sir Rennell, former British ambassador to Italy, head of a commission that had reorganized Egyptian currency, poet and Homeric authority, had listed stopping places all agreed were interesting. In America I had been told that President Hoover had wanted John Garrett to become ambassador to Italy. Before we left Naples, he received word of his appointment. He served with great distinction and became a frequent guest of Victor Emmanuel, many more times than protocol demanded, because of their common interest in numismatics. John had one of the most important collections of ancient coins in America.

September is an ideal month for cruising in the Mediterranean, and we had sunny weather the entire voyage. We heard of one or two *borras* hitting off Cannes and Nice, but we encountered nothing stronger than gentle breezes.

Sir Arthur Evans was still digging and scraping at Knossos when we arrived about the seventh of September. The ladies on the wall of the Fish Room were just beginning to appear in their Bakst-like Minoan costumes, and at Sir Arthur's invitation I was among the first hundred people to sit in what had been Minos' throne. Our party were among the first moderns to stroll down the oldest street in the world. Despite the narrowness that obliged charioteers to pass one another single file, there were sidewalks not unlike modern ones.

At Rhodes, Mussolini's governor had the red carpet waiting for John. The only favorable thing people used to say about Il Duce was that he made trains run on time. He also did something for scholars. The governors of the Dodecanese were all archaeologists with powers to restore whatever seemed worthwhile in their jurisdiction. On Rhodes, the walls of the ancient city had been restored to their condition during the siege of Suleiman the Magnificent in 1520. The Street of the Hospitallers, the ancient Market Place, and Suleiman's Gate had all been repaired, and the thousands of gravestones in the Muslim military cemetery outside the walls were as erect and neat as when Suleiman ordered the burial of his slain warriors. As was customary, Suleiman had a carved turban placed atop each gravestone. If in moonlight one approached the cemetery from the Albergo de la Rosas, one had the eerie panorama of a ghostly army frozen in its march against the beleaguered knights. Almost forty years later I recalled experiencing the illusion and used it in a passage of fantasy in my novel *A Souvenir from Qam*. Our coming to Rhodes again made us *au courant* with recent archaeological finds. Only a week earlier the lovely crouching Venus of Rhodes had been brought up from the sea. When we saw her, she was still encrusted from her centuries of immersion.

Recently, Santorini has been much in the headlines because of its adjacency to what its American discoverers declare is the lost Atlantis. They could not have been more startled by their find than I was when we sailed into Santorini's harbor. All at once I was coeval with the age when the Greeks were creating their theology. I was spellbound by the work of a Titan who, after scooping out a perfectly round basin in the center of an island, had with his finger made an opening through which the sea could fill it, allowing diminutive objects like men and their ships to find a haven.

We anchored in the middle of the harbor and came ashore by the yacht's tender.

Small boats can come ashore at Santorini's level fringe of rock. Donkeys carry you up a steep, narrow, zigzag road to the village of Thera. John and Sir Rennell were engaging donkeys for the climb and Hugh and I were standing a little apart from the others in the party when Santorini's spell touched me again. We did not need words to assure each other we were looking at the most beautiful female either of us had ever seen. In the centuries before their sculpture became anatomically representational, generation after generation of artists had worked toward that arbitrary ideal of a woman's figure wearing a more or less realistic chiton but whose face, while varying slightly in its planes, invariably had the same mouth curving into an obligatory Archaic Smile. Miraculously, we were gazing at a perfect example of that Smile. It was on the face of a little girl of about eight. She herself stood still as a statue between two much younger boys. Her features would have made Praxiteles stare in wonder. Her smile was not an arbitrary flex of muscles on a perfect head, it was the smile of a living child, glimpsing two odd-looking but amusing strangers. We beckoned to Helen Woods and Mary Rogers, who were a few feet away. Hardly moving their bodies, the children observed the two other adults. Unfortunately, I had left my camera on the yacht and could not photograph the lovely child.

We continued on our way, bumping and swaying up the narrow road to Thera. Under white stars we speculated on the age of the handful of houses that made up the community, enjoyed the panoramic view of the incredibly circular harbor, and zigzagged down again to where we had first seen the three children. They had gone and were probably in bed.

Two days later we were at Epidaurus on the Peloponnesus, where we met one of the two or three giants of American photography, Dr. Arnold Genthe. He accepted Alice's invitation to drive back to Nauplia, where the *Sayonara* was anchored, and have dinner with us. He had been spending the summer moving about Greece with his camera, and the results of his labors would be exhibited in the late fall at one of the galleries on Fifty-seventh Street. When we asked his next destination he smiled.

"I am going to a little island called Santorini. It has very few inhabitants, but I am told should be interesting to a photographer."

We barraged him with our pleas to find our small living goddess and, as a master, achieve what I, as a rank amateur, had failed to do. The sequel to our conversation occurred three months later. Alice, John, and Hugh were in Baltimore and the Rodds were in England. Either Helen or Mary, I forget which, had read in the morning paper that an exhibition of photographs Dr. Arnold Genthe had taken in Greece would open that afternoon.

We appeared at the gallery, and at the door we were told that Dr. Genthe was somewhere about. The crowd at the opening was thick, and we could not find him, nor was there any photograph of the Venus of Santorini. We were about to go when I spied Dr. Genthe glaring at us over a small sea of heads. We wormed our way to him. His greeting was anything but cordial.

"I saw you come in," he said, "uninvited. Why did you play such a shabby trick on me?"

We were bewildered.

"What shabby trick?" asked Helen.

"You told me that on Santorini I would find a child of pure classic beauty. Everyone remembered your being there. I spoke to a dozen children who watched you engage donkeys for the climb to Thera, but no one saw the two small boys and the girl child you promised me I would find. You made them up, didn't you?"

I suppose the truth was that the radiant owner of the Archaic Smile and her brothers were the children of a fisherman briefly visiting Santorini. But I like to feel that one day in 1929 some old and prankish divinity wakened momentarily from sleep and decided to give a group of modern mortals a peep at some of those he knew.

On the island of Patmos I was reminded twice of incidents in my own past. One had occurred less than a year before, and it came to mind during a visit to the older of the two monasteries in the Patmos hills. In the Convent of St. John, where its patron saint is said to have written the

Book of Revelation, the abbot produced many of the monastery's treasures for our admiration. The most valued was a fourth-century transcript of the Book of Revelation. It was on purple vellum. All its lettering was silver except the name of God, which was copied in gold. The abiding grief of the monastery was the absence of a few pages that vandals had stolen sometime, the abbot thought, in the seventeenth century.

You would have a hard time finding anyone who knows less about vellum manuscripts than I do, yet as the abbot meticulously turned the volume's leaves I had a prompting of memory. I looked up and met Helen Woods's eye. Our exchanged glances communicated a bit of knowledge we shared. The missing pages were in the great library Helen's grandfather had built at Madison Avenue and Thirty-fifth; fewer than six months earlier Belle Green, the Morgan librarian, had shown them to me. I saw them again a few years ago when Freddie Addams, the present librarian, had them on view in a glass case for the edification of members and guests at an annual meeting of the Morgan Fellows.

Again I had come ashore without my camera, and I left our group and footed it down to Patmos' shallow harbor. I waved a handkerchief signal for the tender and strolled over to a nearby *taverna*, where I intended to wait for the tender's arrival. A young man in his late twenties seated at one of the outdoor tables came over to mine and greeted me politely in English. He asked if he could be of any assistance. He agreed to help me drink some Greek beer. I asked if he was a native of Patmos.

"I was born here, sir," he replied, "and I have been visiting my parents, who live in the mountains. I came to town today to see if I could get some news on the Pirates."

I was startled. "Pirates, in the Aegean?"

"Oh, no, sir, the Pittsburgh Pirates. When I saw your yacht I thought you might possibly have some recent American newspapers on board."

There was a sequel to that meeting, too. When I was trying out *The Farmer Takes a Wife* in Washington, D.C., in 1937 after a Wednesday matinée I invited June Walker, one of the play's stars, to have a drink with me in the cocktail bar of the Hotel Washington. On our way there from the theater I introduced, with seeming casualness, the incident of my encounter with the baseball fan on Patmos. We reached the hotel and were seated at a table when the headwaiter approached to take our order. I kept him waiting as I reached the climax of my story.

"And would you believe it," I said, "it turned out that the young man had worked in Pittsburgh as a busboy at the Pittsburgh Athletic Association when I was there and he probably helped lay the table where I used to sit."

"Golly," said June, "you must have been surprised!"

"I was," I said, "and I'm going to give you one. Meet Mr. Varos, who's been standing here laughing. He was the young man."

I explained that Mr. Varos had recognized me at dinner the night before and had reminded me of our first encounter.

After cruising through the Greek waters and the Corinth Canal, we sailed for Italy.

As everyone says, one sees Venice at its best by arriving at twilight. It is quite true. Turner would have appreciated the after-sunset glow that dyed the city when we dropped anchor there for the last time. In her ducal palazzo on the Grand Canal the fabulous Princess Polignac, the Singer heiress who financed the original production of *Noces* and other Diaghilev ballets, welcomed us with a party of a lavishness unusual even for her because, she said, we were the first yachting party in several years that had disbanded with all its members still good friends.

During the voyage, I had spent many hours between shore visits polishing scenes in *The Green Pastures*. The cruise, with its constant enjoyments, had an added savor when one evening off the island of Samos, Alice invited me to read the play. For the first time I read it aloud to a group of listeners. Their reaction was a tonic to me, and when I returned to New York I was surer than ever that despite managerial discouragement the play had merit. October and November went by with my scripts still on the shelf. I completed the two remaining comedy scripts due RKO, whose earnings with the returns from a few magazine pieces added to a very small working capital. Certainly it was not enough to permit any investment in stocks. When people began jumping out of windows at the end of November I had lost nothing in the Wall Street crash and as an onlooker found myself admiring the grace with which George Kaufman, F.P.A., Woollcott, Ross, and others met the general disaster.

On the first of December I did not share the common woe in anticipating Christmas. The likelihood of any manager, or anyone else for that matter, having enough money to produce my play could not have been more dim. It was then, by a happy chance, that I met Rowland Stebbins. Mr. Stebbins had been a Wall Street broker gifted with a kind of extrasensory perception. He had disposed of his personal wagonload of blue-chip stocks at the moment of their greatest value, before the boom collapsed. With Wall Street flat on its back, he decided that the theater district would be a pleasanter neighborhood to spend his time and money. He and George Kaufman were frequent fellow bridgeplayers at the Cavendish Club. He asked George if he had any uncommitted playscripts. George said he didn't but that I had a play George thought was good despite its many rejections. The next day Stebbins' business manager arrived at my apartment to pick up the script.

Two days later I met Broadway's new angel. Enthusiastically he said he would like to produce the play as soon as I could put it on the stage. Not knowing then that he was as astutely foresighted as he was fortunate, I told him what I would have told anyone not aware of the hazards implicit in *The Green Pastures*. I told him that more than one friendly manager had cautioned me about the enormous risk of disfavor that was likely to arise over a play in which God was depicted as a Negro. It was possible, I said, that the producer as well as the author might go to jail for their temerity. Finally, for my conscience' sake, I had to say he must not expect any motion-picture company to have the faintest interest in it. The only part of my warning that concerned him was the possible charge of sacrilege.

"Of course, there are bigots everywhere," he agreed, "and I can imagine some of them wanting to burn us at the stake. I can see those with political pressure running us out of Philadelphia, Boston, and other cities on a rail. If it's all right with you, let's not think of any out-of-town tryouts and open right here in New York."

Basic considerations were solved before the week was out. Robert Edmond Jones was free and eager to develop the rough sketches already made for sets and costumes. Rowland suggested that Hall Johnson make the vocal arrangements of the spirituals and conduct their singing by his well-known choir. Miriam Doyle of Rowland's staff would supervise the costumes that would be made from Jones's designs. Inquiries were begun to find a theater with a stage large enough to accommodate the unusual load of scenery and two wide treadmills that would be important to the play's action. An Actors' Equity rule permitted no more than four weeks' rehearsal for a "straight" play. Musicals were allowed five. I appeared before the Equity Council, explained the unusual nature of our production, and was granted the extra week. Although we were still without a theater, the quick solution of the preliminary preparations led us to decide that if we started casting immediately, the principal actors would be selected within the next three weeks.

With our five weeks' rehearsals, we could start on December 29 and open on Wednesday, February 26. From the moment I met him, Rowland demonstrated that he had a genuine flair for production. According to the provisions of the Dramatists' Guild contract, the final authority on the casting of plays rests with the author. As a rule he and the play's director chose the performers. In nine cases out of ten Rowland and I agreed in our selections. I was delighted when Rowland said he would like to be with me when I interviewed the Negroes to be among our one hundred performers. Our press agent, the gentle William Fields, who in later years headed the publicity staff of Barnum and Bailey, Ringling Brothers Circus, sent out the announcements that *The Green Pastures,* a play with an all-Negro cast, was about to go into rehearsal.

There were no official statistics to prove it, but it was said that Harlem's population included ten thousand actors and actresses, dancers and other entertainers. The next day, and for weeks after, the streets around the offices of John Carey's casting agency on 132nd Street were jammed with applicants. In front of the Lafayette Theater on Seventh Avenue at 131st Street grew what every Harlemite knew as the Tree of Hope. It was an ordinary plane tree but was reported to be of infallible aid if you touched its trunk and prayed for work. Before rehearsals started for *The Green Pastures* I was told its bark was almost worn off.

Through the inner office in which Rowland and I considered candidates poured an endless stream of men and women whose work was known to Carey and his manager, Pat Burk, and seemed to them suitable for different roles. I, too, was aware of the talent of several well-known players. One of the first contracts was made with Wesley Hill, a splendid actor who had shown great artistry as the Jake, the fisherman in DuBose Heyward's *Porgy.* If you are old enough you may remember the poignant scene in which he held his tiny son in the air listening to warnings not to face an approaching storm. Love and pride, but no anxiety were in his: "How this man-child goin' to get a college education if I don't go to sea?"

I felt he might be a magnificent Angel Gabriel.

Within the next few days dozens of other actors also

of proven accomplishment, were selected to play other parts. Filling the role of De Lawd was difficult. The actor had to be physically big, have a bearing not only dignified but noble, and a voice rich with quiet authority and capable of thunderous wrath. The agent, Rowland and I, and friends from whom we begged help, could recall no actor who could fill even an approximation of those requirements. Half a dozen sugggested candidates who had acted in the theater and now lived in southern states were brought North. One or two were summoned from Chicago. All bore little resemblance to De Lawd we were seeking.

A week before rehearsals were to start reported progress was being made by Bobby Jones and Miriam on scenery and costumes. Danny Murphy, a tireless property man, and his assistants were assembling the myriad of props necessary. For the fish fry, Danny had found a basket of lifelike rubber catfish, and, to augment real ones, triangular wooden sandwiches with inviting jam fillings painted on their sides. (I still have a few of them and they are still tempting.) He had not yet been able to find a walking stick that Moses could turn into a snake, but he was sure he would have one by the time rehearsals reached the scene in Pharaoh's court where it would be used.

We had even got a theater, one with a big enough stage to present the more spectacular scenes without cramping. It was The Mansfield, a fine structure built by the Chanin brothers before the market crash. It had thus far housed nothing but flops. Its manager for the Chanins, Harry Kline, was an old friend. As all but one or two theaters in New York were feeling the first pain of the Depression, he was willing to accept *The Green Pastures* as a tenant. The guarantee of two weeks' occupancy at a good rental was better than nothing.

It was a cold, dismal morning, four days before the rehearsals were scheduled to start, when Rowland and I started our routine trek to Harlem. The day before, we had engaged the last of the sixteen small fry who would appear as cherubs and members of the Sunday school class. One was the small son of a woman who was to play the First Lady Angel and the free-speaking Second Cleaner in God's office. She was a professional, and she assured me like a classic stage mother that her little boy was too. This was attested by the business card she gave me which read:

JAZZLIPS RICHARDSON, JR.
THE WONDER CHILD

Our taxi crept slowly northward through sleet and snow. It seemed as spiritless as we were. The prospect of another day of hopeless search for the one man without whom there would be no production was grim. In near-desperation Rowland had tried to persuade Dr. Adam Clayton Powell, Sr., the congressman's distinguished father, to leave his five thousand parishioners in the outstanding Abyssinian Baptist Church in New York to play De Lawd. Dr. Powell had the physical characteristics the part needed. He had liked the play but declined to leave the pulpit for the stage.

When we arrived at the agency, the agent had a scattering of new faces for us to see. Desperately we tried to picture one as improving with voice lessons, another at least a little bit taller with shoe lifts, this one's scanty hair covered with a wig, or padding on a tall, scarecrow-like figure. When the last one had been thanked for coming,

Rowland and I were wordless, silently plumbing new ocean-like depths of depression. Then the casting agent came in from the outer office.

"I've got an old fellow here I just heard about the other day. He's not an actor, but he's done some reading in schools and certainly looks like what we're after."

Spiritlessly we told the casting agent to show him in.

In *Here Are Ladies* James Stephens says: "God came down the street like a man and a half." In a dingy cubbyhole of an office Richard Berry Harrison appeared with similar dimensions. Topping his six-foot height was a head of leonine gray hair. Below it, we saw a face that had managed to weather sixty-five years of struggle and disheartenment. It was a face maturely serene because of the dauntless inner strength of the gentle being who wore it. He spoke with a voice like a cello's. Gravely and courteously he said he had heard we were looking for actors and that he had been told he might be right for a part.

Mr. Harrison agreed to read the play that night. The next morning he telephoned that he had read the play. He had found himself agreeing that a great many Negroes interpreted the Bible the way the people in the play did. He was doubtful of his qualifications to play De Lawd. It was true, he said, that in Negro schools about the country he had read scenes from Shakespeare's plays and recited the poems of Paul Laurence Dunbar, who, he told me, had been best man at his wedding. He also questioned his ability to learn to speak in the dialect of the Deep South because his speech was acquired in Montreal, where he had been born. As the religious grandson of slaves who had fled from Alabama to Canada by way of the Underground

Railroad, he had a final and much more serious question that must be answered.

"I know you weren't trying to make fun of my people when you wrote the play, Mr. Connelly, but I wouldn't like to do something that might make Negroes feel I'd let them down. I just don't know what to do."

I felt certain De Lawd's way of talking would not be difficult for him to learn and that with five weeks' hard work he would be completely at ease on the stage. His last anxiety was not easy to allay. One of Rowland's intimate friends was Herbert Shipman, the Suffragan Bishop of New York. Rowland had consulted him after reading the play and been assured that if it were properly produced it might be enjoyed by people of any creed. Mr. Harrison had told us he was an Episcopalian and agreed to let Bishop Shipman talk with him about the play and help him decide whether or not to play it. Bishop Shipman broke an engagement to talk with Mr. Harrison that night. The next morning Rowland told me the Bishop had called him after a long discussion with his conscientious caller.

"I don't know whether he'll do it or not," the Bishop said guardedly. "We talked about *The Green Pastures* for almost two hours, and in spite of the bumps he has had from life, he is an unworldly man. A fine man with a conscience that has guided him all his life. He listened attentively to everything I had to say, but he said that before he made up his mind he wanted to go home and pray over the problem. He promised to call you this morning."

At eleven o'clock I was in Rowland's office when Mr. Harrison kept his promise.

"Good morning, Mr. Connelly, this is Richard Harrison." As if I could have mistaken that cello voice for anyone else's.

"Good morning, Mr. Harrison. I hear you had a good talk with Bishop Shipman."

"I did. I had a long talk with him last night. He is a very fine gentleman."

"He thought highly of you, too," I said. "Well"—and never was there such false casualness in a *well*—"have you decided if you are going to be with us?"

He responded with some of the finest tones a cello ever played: "I hope I can be with you right along, Mr. Connelly."

So forty-eight hours before those in the play would begin rehearsals by listening to a reading of it, Rowland and I came as close to uttering a prayer of thanks as a couple of agnostics could.

Shortly after *The Green Pastures* opened, several southern newspapers screamed their editorial indignation at the outrageous sacrilege contained in a play in New York they had no intention of seeing. The editor of the Richmond *Courier* did not join the blasts of bigotry, but he was mad enough to come to New York and see for himself just how vile a play could be. When he returned home he filled two editorial columns with hosannas. He described every scene in detail. When he came to Mr. Harrison's first entrance he wrote:

"Then out on the stage came the finest-looking old man I have ever seen."

Even as late as 1929 it was difficult to rent space in the Broadway area in which to rehearse plays with Negro casts. Every Broadway stage but one was denied *The Green Pastures*. The exception was the tiny Belmont on

Forty-eighth Street on the fringe of Times Square. Its stage was small, and because our cast numbered almost a hundred only those scenes employing a handful of players could be rehearsed on it. We ran through the lines of ensemble scenes with the cast sitting in the orchestra chairs.

The last two weeks of rehearsals were in Bryant Hall on Sixth Avenue opposite Bryant Park. The building must have been built before the Civil War. Once it had provided several floors of elegant assembly rooms. By the late twenties it was a dilapidated warren for performers in every branch of professional entertainment. Day and night through thin walls came the noisy bedlam of musical comedy choruses, jazz bands, and other groups rehearsing. Floors sagged under the pounding feet of dancers and acrobats. The pungent smells of disinfectants failed to subdue the building's permanent odor of decay. Wintry gusts jostled drafty windows. The clanking steam radiators did not provide as much heat as the bodies of the hall's tenants.

Despite the physical discomforts, cheerfulness dominated our own quarters on the second floor. As a rule actors guard themselves against optimism during rehearsals. Our opening night was still two weeks away when I found the traditional discretion being blithely ignored at least by some of the cast.

The company was reassembling after an evening dinner break. On the landing outside our rehearsal hall a cluster of the younger actors were listening at the open door of a telephone booth. I heard someone in it say:

"April when? . . . No, we got a matinee that day. How about that Friday? . . . O.K., check. . . . The next open date? Lemme look in the book. . . . Not till July. . . . OK. You call us later."

It was the manager of *The Green Pastures* baseball team booking playing dates for the summer.

Mr. Harrison's inexperience as an actor proved to be no handicap in building his characterization and in his learning the mechanics of movements. The difference between good acting and bad lies in the fact that a good actor "acts" about one-tenth as much as a poor one. Instinctively, Mr. Harrison recognized that economy of physical movement is of vital importance. Most of his line readings had exactly the right intonations and projections. Those he changed were edited properly with little or no difficulty. Because as an elocutionist he knew the danger of the superfluous gesture, there was never need to tell him that one of the most vital assets in an actor's performance is repose. I quickly discovered that all one needed to do to help him with physical movements about the stage was to explain them in the simplest mechanical terms. In the first scene in God's office Mr. Harrison was uncertain of the suiting of actions to words.

"When you ask Gabriel what time it is by the sun and the stars, let him look out of the window alone and just think of where you're going to begin your walk on Earth. Then when He says, 'Jest exactly half-past, Lawd,' turn slowly toward the hat rack by the door and as you say, 'O.K. You take care of yourself, Gabriel. I'll be back Saturday,' you're reaching for your hat so that you're lifting it from the hook on the word 'Saturday.' " In half a minute Mr. Harrison was doing it perfectly. And in public performance his seeming casualness never failed to evoke affectionate laughter from audiences.

Mr. Harrison had one fear about his competence which my constant reassurances did little to allay. He questioned his ability to learn his part within the five weeks' rehearsal period. He felt a bit easier when I told him that instead of the customary single prompter, I would have at least three so that one would always be close to any area on stage where he would be playing a scene.

As is customary, the first days of rehearsal had been given to line readings by the seated cast as they familiarized themselves with the script. On the third reading there was an increase in the murmuring that had occurred during one of Mr. Harrison's speeches in the play's second half. It was a part of a scene I hoped would be poignantly appealing but which I did not expect to cause any reaction while being rehearsed.

At his office window in heaven, God is torn between wrath and compassion as He hears the prayers from the Earth He has abandoned. The lines I had written for his capitulation included, "I ain't comin' down to help you. I'm jest in de dozens and wanta feel a little better, dat's all." I asked Tutt Whitney, who played Noah, why the speech was causing audible reactions. He answered with a whisper of embarrassment:

"Maybe you don't know what 'in de dozens' means."

I said I had heard it spoken by colored people in Louisiana and that saying "in the dozens" meant one was greatly depressed, feeling the bluest of the blues. Tutt was surprised.

"Oh, that's not what it means in Harlem." He hunted for a polite phrase. "You say it when someone is sleeping with his aunt."

On learning that a lamentation in the South was a confession of incest in the North, I quickly rewrote the speech.

Another memorable incident occurred one evening toward the end of rehearsals when I joined one of the women chorusers climbing the sleet-covered steps from the sidewalk to the entrance of Bryant Hall. Despite her several weeks' attendance, she had not familiarized herself with anything except her vocal part in the choir. Silently we climbed the steps together. At the doorway, she timidly tugged at the sleeve of my overcoat.

"Mr. Connelly," she ventured hesitantly, "can I ask you a question?"

"Of course. What is it?"

With innocent curiosity she asked, "When are we going to shoot this picture?"

Rowland Stebbins' constant enthusiasm with the progress of rehearsals was dampened when he came to watch. In the draft of the play which had made him want to be its producer, the scene in which David killed Goliath had called for the presence of David's victim. Before being toppled over by David's sling, his victim would have to be seen only to the knees, the rest of him toppling offstage, his six-foot-long shoes rising vertically at his demise. The scene ended with a regathering of David's scattered sheep while the Sweet Singer of Israel resumed his interrupted singing of "Little David Play on Yo' Harp."

Rowland had been a frequent visitor at rehearsals. They had been underway about two weeks when after a long day's session we adjourned to The Players Club for a midnight snack. He asked me with concern, "When are you going to rehearse the Little David scene?"

I must have seemed a bit casual as I looked up from my Welsh rarebit. "Oh, that scene's out."

Rowland stared. "Out? Out? Why that's just about my favorite scene in the play." He was appalled, and a fork fell from his hand to his plate. "Why, dammit, that scene was one of the reasons I decided to *do* the play!"

I saw that the *camaraderie* we had been sharing for months had grown icy. "I'm sorry, Rowland," I said. "It's a scene I like very much too. It happens to have been one that I wrote as an experiment even before I began to dialogue the rest of the play."

Rowland stared at me, incredulous. "Then—why—why—"

"Because it's gratuitous. It doesn't fit into the script. I'd like to see it played as much as you would, and if you can tell me where it can go without completely destroying the continuity I'll put it in the works."

Rowland was stunned. He reached for the working script in which I intended to study the day's minor changes before going to bed. His glass of ale grew flat as he examined scene after scene. At last he closed the covers and looked up at me with a hesitant, self-reproachful smile.

"I guess you're right," he said, and that was the one and only time Little David's absence from the play was discussed.

My own affection for the Little David scene has never diminished. Ray Long heard of its deletion and published it in *Cosmopolitan*, which he was then editing, and it has been produced by puppeteers in America and Europe but never in a production of the play.

This was the way I wrote it:

LITTLE DAVID

The scene is a grassy glade. Mechanical sheep are grazing up-stage. Sunlight dapples the scene through the trees. David, a little Negro boy, enters. He is barefooted and, besides his long switch, carries a homemade guitar. He seats himself on a rock.

DAVID. Hello, sheep an' lambs. Wanter hear little David sing?

[*The sheep look up.* DAVID *begins to sing.*]

Oh, Joshua was de son of Nun
He nevah quit wukk to his wukk was done.
Little David, play on yo' hawp,
Hallelu, hallelu,
Little David, Play on yo' hawp,
Hallelu.

[*During the next verse the approximation of a wolf appears over a rise in the background. The sheep scatter to the right and left, but the wolf catches one and drags it out of sight.*]

Ol' Noah he did build de Awk
An' he build it out of poplar bawk.
Little David, play on yo' hawp,
Hallelu, hallelu,
Little David, play on yo' hawp,
Hal—

[*The song is broken by the bleating of the attacked sheep.* DAVID *turns and sees the wolf disappearing. He jumps up.*]

Well, dog-gone dat ol' wolf. Dat's do fo'th sheep dis week he's tooken. I gotter stop dat. I gotter figure some way to ruin dat wolf. [*He sits, somewhat in the attitude of Rodin's "Penseur."*] I gotter invent somethin'. [*He thinks for a moment; then smiles.*] I's invented it. [*He reaches to the ground and picks up a piece of cord.*] Diss'll do it. It's jest de right invention. C'm on back, sheep an' lambs. He ain't gonter hurt you no mo'. [*The sheep timidly return.*] Now you jest fool aroun' an' make out like things is goin' along jest as usual.

> [*He resumes singing, but this time he does not play his guitar. He holds the sling in readiness, and warily watches for the approach of the wolf.*]

> De Lawd picked out ol' Abraham,
> Wild as a lion, meek as a lamb.
> Little David, play on yo' hawp,
> Hallelu, hallelu,
> Little David, play on yo' hawp,
> Hallelu.

> [*The wolf stealthily comes into sight again.* DAVID *senses his presence but continues to sing.*]

> De Lawd got mad, set de world on fiah,
> Burned up Sol'mun an' Gomiah,
> Little David, play on yo' hawp,
> Hallelu, hallelu,
> Little David, play on yo' hawp,
> Halleeee—

> [*The wolf is about to take another sheep. David turns swiftly and casts the sling. The wolf leaps in the air and falls over the rise in the distance.*]

Wham! Don't need be 'fraid now, lambs an' sheep. [*He examines the sling. Then goes upstage to see the wolf.*] Dat's a good invention. Who's dis comin' along? Doggone, he looks like he's drunk.

> [*The* PROPHET SAMUEL *appears. He is an elderly Negro, greatly bewildered.*]

SAMUEL. Who dat? Why, it's little David. Oh, little David, de Lawd's pronounced a jedgment. I'm so out of my mind, I've been tearin' across fields every whichaway, not knowin' where I was goin'.

DAVID. What's de Lawd done?

SAMUEL. Ain't you been home lately, son?

DAVID. I've been out yere fo' two weeks.

SAMUEL. David, de Philistines is captured us, an' yere we is goin' into bondage ag'in.

DAVID. [*Appalled.*] Oh, no!

SAMUEL. Dey ain't no use talkin'. Dey's burnin' our cities right now.

DAVID. But dey can't take our town.

SAMUEL. Dey moved in dis mo'nin'.

DAVID. But my three brothers is dere, Granddaddy Samuel. Dey wouldn't *let* 'em take it!

SAMUEL. We's got de Lawd mad ag'in, little David, an' nobody kin stop 'em. Yo' three brothers was killed by deir head man jest a little bit ago.

DAVID. My brothers is de stoutest men in de whole land of Canaan. What did dey do? Take him on one at a time, wid deir han's tied?

SAMUEL. He beat all three to once wid *his* han's tied an' his feet shackled. He's so strong it looked like he jest breathed 'em down. It looks like de end of Israel too, little David. [SAMUEL *gazes offstage toward the ruined town.*]

DAVID. No. 'Count caize de Lawd loves us. I know dat, 'count caize he likes de songs I made up. He's tol' me so.

SAMUEL. Look, dere's our little town burnin'. Deir big head man took it all by hisself.

DAVID. [*Simply.*] I kin whup him. I got de means.

SAMUEL. [*Still looking away.*] I knew we was offendin' de Lawd. I tried to make us stop. He give us dis pretty Land of Canaan, an' look what we've done wid it?

DAVID. [*Inspired.*] I kin whup him. I got de means.

SAMUEL. [*Still inattentive.*] An' now de Chosen People is abandoned. De deliverer was to come, but—[*He turns slowly, puzzled.*] What did you say, little David?

DAVID. [*His eyes on the sky above.*] I kin whup him. I got de means.

[SAMUEL *stares, then goes to him.*]

SAMUEL. [*Softly, in awe.*] Wid what?

DAVID. [*Showing the sling.*] Wid dis.

SAMUEL. Little David!

[DAVID *lowers his eyes and turns to* SAMUEL.]

DAVID. What?

SAMUEL. I believe you kin do it! [*Excitedly.*] Yes, suh. Why de way yo' standin' dere is jest de way I always pictured de Lawd's anointed. Fo' fo'ty years I been lookin' fo' him. *Dat's* why I went 'cross de fields dat crazy way! I thought I was losin' my min'. But no, dat wuz de Lawd's wukk. Little David, he was leadin' me right yere to you all de time!

DAVID. De Lawd's on our side still.

SAMUEL. [*Almost shouting.*] Co'se he is! We gonter be saved! Go git 'em, little David! Thank you, Lawd, fo' lettin' me find him. [SAMUEL *starts to leave.*]

DAVID. Whar you goin', Granddaddy Samuel?

SAMUEL. I'm gonter spread de news. I'm goin' to de temple an' den tell ol' King Saul what he wants to hear.

DAVID. [*A little surprised.*] You gonter tell him what I said?

SAMUEL. I'm gonter tell all Israel de deliverer's been found. Dat it wasn't nobody on earth but little David. Dat it was little David all de time. An' now at las', he's took charge!

[SAMUEL *leaves.* DAVID *lowers his head.*]

DAVID. Tell me what to do, Lawd.

[THE LORD *appears over the rise.*]

THE LORD. Do what comes into yo' mind, David.

DAVID. [*Still in prayer.*] Yes, Lawd.

THE LORD. I was pretty near ready to give mankind up. But I'm gonter give 'em dis one las' chance, David, on 'count of you.

DAVID. Yes, Lawd.

THE LORD. I'm gonter make you de king. You is gonter be my sweet singer. If dey break my laws ag'in I'm gonter abandon dem fo'ever. You be a good king, David, an' teach 'em dat.

David. Yes, Lawd.

The Lord. Yere comes ol' Goliath. He's de biggest man dey got. I 'spect he heard yo' defy. You give it to him, David. An' give it to him good. [The Lord *disappears.*]

> [*From the other side of the stage come the legs of* Goliath. *That part of him above the knees is hidden from sight. He stops.* David *picks up a stone and puts it in the sling.*]

Goliath's Voice. Whar at's dat little boy dat's talkin' so big?

David. I'm him.

Goliath's Voice. You? Why, you ain't no bigger dan a little bug.

David. Mebbe so. Dat don't mean nothin'!

Goliath's Voice. It do when I jine de party. Does you know who I am?

David. Yo' ol' Goliath.

Goliath's Voice. Dat's it. An' I'm de biggest an' stoutest man in de worl'! Me, I'm so strong dat toornadoes an' harricanes follow me 'round' like little peg dogs, I spits lightnin' an' I breathes thunder, an' I'm de doom of Israel.

David. All de same I take notice you got sweat on yo' brow.

Goliath's Voice. I jest walked through a cloud. Dat's only de wetness.

David. Well, yere's somethin' else fo' yo' brow. [*He casts the sling.*]

Goliath's Voice. Now, what you tryin' to do down dere? Tease me? I'spect I better jest bend over an' flick you down once an' fo'— Oooh!

> [*The body of* Goliath *falls. That is, the legs topple back, the knees offstage, and the shoes of the late giant come up perpendicularly about the center of the stage.*]

David. Wham!

> [*He goes to the feet. The sheep, which had run away at* Goliath's *approach, timidly reappear.* David *in-*

*spects the fallen body, shading his eyes with his hand
as he looks off at the distant head.*]

Right in de middle o' de fo'head

[*He smiles, then picks up his guitar, and resting his
left elbow in the cup of Goliath's downstage heel,
begins to sing again.*]

Oh, David was a shepherd boy.
He killed Goliath an' hollered fo' joy.
Little David—

[*The light grows brighter. The choir offstage joins
in the singing and the sheep begin to dance.*]

—play on yo' hawp,
Hallelu, hallelu,
Little David, play on yo' hawp,
Hallelu!

CURTAIN

During the last week of rehearsals a minor problem
rose that could have been solved quickly if I had been
more imaginative as a director. Bobby Jones's genius had
met the challenge of nineteen changes of scenes so that
they flowed from one to another with speed and smoothness. The hundreds of costumes he had designed were being realized by Miriam Doyle and her corps of tailors and
seamstresses. The completely correct black frock coat for
De Lawd was discovered in a second-hand clothing store
on Seventh Avenue. Danny Murphy, a king among prop-
ertymen, had found the perfect ornately covered volume
from which the *Rev. Deshee* would read parts of the First
Book of Moses to his Sunday school class. It is one of the
souvenirs of the first production that I treasure. Pasted in

its early pages are Mr. Deshee's typewritten lines. They were there not merely to facilitate Charles H. Moore's performance. A real clergyman would have been unable to find a passage between the Pentateuch and Revelation. Danny Murphy, in achieving the perfect book cover for the Sunday school lectern had obtained not a book of Scriptures but a very handsomely bound copy of *A History of Ireland*.

The big quandary Danny faced for several days was not overcome until the last minute, actually the afternoon before the play's premiere. The transformation of Aaron's rod into the snake at the foot of Pharaoh's throne had been insuperable until the eleventh-hour construction of an invisible mechanism that made the rod wiggle at the proper moment. Danny was justifiably pleased with his accomplishment. It wasn't until I staged a revival of the play in 1952 that the cane-into-snake incident found a solution that might have saved Danny Murphy hours of travail. Instead of the help of a mechanical device I directed Frank Wilson, who was playing Moses, to place the rod of Aaron on the throne's step. Then, by including the entire court in a sweep of his arm, hypnotize them into believing what they could not see. Dramatically it was an effective employment of one of the "tricks" De Lawd had taught Moses.

After a single day's rehearsal the mass of scenery, the complex lighting plot, and two forty-foot treadmills that would have to carry a hundred marchers in the Exodus scene all promised to function properly. The last-minute alterations in costumes were negligible. On February 25, the day before the play's premiere, we had two full dress rehearsals. The three prompters I had promised Mr. Harrison had to be coached to avoid collisions with stagehands and scenery during the split-second changes. For many days, as was to be expected, the cast, with the exception of Mr. Harrison, was letter-perfect. At the last week of rehearsals he too had been quite at ease, playing every scene excellently. He had fluffed nothing when adjusting himself to the employment of props, not even the double duty of sketching for Noah the specifications of the ark while vocally building to a passionate dramatic climax the details of the Flood. At the last afternoon rehearsal the hundred marchers in the Exodus scene had to repeat it several times before Walter Lommatzsch and his crew of electricians adjusted the speed of the treadmills to the heavy weight of those using it. At the final rehearsal that night the voltage and weight had been nicely balanced, but Mr. Harrison's lone employment of the treadmill in the scene leading to his encounter with Noah produced another problem. Walking on a moving platform with steps which, to an audience, would seem a natural pace, and occasionally stopping simultaneously, with the treadmill to talk with the human beings he encountered proved so difficult that he had to be aided verbally from the wings.

Despite my assurances that he was improving with each repetition his distress was great when I stopped the rehearsal so that he might sit down. Long after midnight I sat with him in his dressing room promising that he would be comfortable and competent after we had rehearsed his treadmill scenes again the following afternoon. After he had gone I read my notes to the rest of the company and excused all but three or four of the principals and told most of the company they could rest until it was time to report for the opening-night performance. Those I had excepted I asked to appear at noon for last-minute polishing of their scenes.

Mr. Harrison was to resume tackling the treadmill at 2 P.M.

He arrived promptly, apparently refreshed and if not overconfident, determined to do his best. In less than an hour he had coordinated walking, stopping, and speaking to a point where prompting was no longer required. He promised to go home and rest before the performance.

Until a few minutes before curtain time I stayed in the theater, going over minor technical uncertainties with Jack Curtis, the chief stage manager, Claude Archer, his first assistant, and Eddie Gardner, who had supervised the lighting. When we left the theater for a quick snack before curtain time we knew that by forgoing an out-of-town tryout we were facing hazards no spectacular theatrical production as intricately demanding as ours had ever before faced.

When the curtain rose on that crucial night I stood in the rear of the Mansfield so attentive to the play's technical operation I had no time for playwright's jitters.

The children in the Sunday school scene at the play's start won the audience immediately. I had told them not to speak should there be laughter at anything they said or did. The laughs they heard were frequent and loud. Like seasoned troupers they waited for them to die.

The scene faded on cue, and in the darkness Hall Johnson's magnificent choir burst into the first of the many entre-scene spirituals. Without a hitch, the lights went up on "The Fish Fry in Heaven." I held my breath as Mr. Harrison made his first entrance. At both of yesterday's rehearsals he had indicated professional ease. I hoped that the knowledge that he was about to face more than a thousand first-nighters would not shake the calm he must maintain. Wesley Hill, in the strikingly beautiful purple and gold vestments Bobby had designed for Gabriel, silenced the celestial picnickers with his cry of: "Gangway! Gangway for De Lawd God Jehovah!" Completely at ease, Mr. Harrison silently entered, went to the center of the stage, and calmly uttered the first line of his greeting to his angels and cherubim. From the moment he began, he had the audience in his pocket. The risk of putting a black God on the stage vanished completely as Mr. Harrison's talent, dignity, rich voice, and gentle, endearing humor flooded auditorium and balcony.

When the scene ended with God's creation of Man it was evident that because of the audience's affectionate responses there would be no recurrence of Richard Berry Harrison's pre-performance stage-fright.

His interview with Adam and Eve in the next scene plus his grieving advice to Cain unfolded with perfect timing and effect.

Other than his trouble with the treadmill Mr. Harrison's only difficulty had been in synchronizing his lines with the many small bits of business in the first of the scenes in De Lawd's office. However, as I had the prompters within whispering distance behind his desk, the office door, and crouching below the upstage window, I knew he felt protected. Unexpectedly, in the middle of the scene there was a break in the rhythm of his talk with Gabriel. Later I was assured it had not been noticed by those in the audience. Two other things they did not notice were that the fluffed line had been one of Gabriel's and that it had been Harrison acting publicly for the first time in his life who, unruffled and *sotto voce*, threw the veteran Wesley Hill his forgotten line.

With incredible smoothness, subsequent scenes followed one after another. I was dumbfounded by our good luck. Just before the curtain fell at the end of the first half I dashed backstage to congratulate the stage crew and the cast. I found Mr. Harrison completely at ease and happy over the audience's responses.

Reports from the lobby of the first-nighters' intermission comments were heartening. After they returned to their seats I waited until the house lights had gone down and returned to the rear of the auditorium. From the moment the curtain's rise disclosed two lady angels dusting furniture in God's office, the mood of the audience was all a playwright could wish. As the act progressed I was in a state of near-bliss, I watched the consistently flawless work of the crew and, to my mind, an inspired cast. As we approached the last scene it seemed apparent that sixty-five-year-old Richard Berry Harrison, the unknown and untried, was achieving a glorious, unparalleled success. When the subdued, somber light disclosed the second fish fry that would end the play, God was surrounded by saints and seraphim brooding on the dignity he had at last found in man. In less than two minutes the curtain would fall.

Now there was little likelihood of even a negligible blunder. I had found a place to sit halfway up the stairs that led to the balcony seats. Stebbens, radiant, joined me.

"How do you feel?" he whispered joyfully.

I was still watching the performance. Exactly on cue the darkened stage blazed with light and the Heavenly Choir began its final song. I started to say I was the happiest man on earth. At that moment a tidal wave of horror rushed down on me. I struggled to my feet. Stebbens was staring at me speechless with dread.

"I must have lost my mind this afternoon!" I gasped. I raced down the aisle and got through a door to the stage just as the descending curtain touched the floor. The explosion of applause and cheers from out front indicated that we had completely won the audience. But I had recognized that in the tension of my preoccupation with other concerns during the last forty-eight hours I had stupidly failed to perform the final obligation of every stage director. I had forgotten to lay out and rehearse curtain calls! Now a potential triumph could turn into a spectacle of idiotic confusion.

A hundred uncertain and bewildered actors stood in the groupings on which the curtain had fallen. I rushed onstage.

"Hold your positions!" I shouted. "We'll have time between the curtains to arrange the bows." I signaled Jack Curtis, and the curtain went up on the full company. Half a dozen times we took "picture" curtain calls. Because the applause never stopped, I was able to keep the curtain down long enough to improvise groupings of the principals. It must have gone up and down on a dozen of these. Now the audience began yelling for De Lawd, Gabriel, Noah, Moses, and others. Fortunately, the curtain was the "tableau" kind, which, when down, could be parted in the center, allowing individual actors to come onto the stage apron. I don't remember how many times I stood behind it sending out Mr. Harrison and a score of other principals for personal accolades. I was becoming numb with the immensity of the play's reception.

Suddenly I found myself being lifted off my feet. Husky Daniel L. Haynes, who had played Adam and Hezdrel, with two more actors as big as himself, were carrying me through the opening in the curtain. For a moment I stood before it in a stupor. Expecting a speech, the audience grew quiet. There stirred in my mind the recollection of the firm conviction George Kaufman and I shared about playwrights who habitually make opening-night speeches. I managed to find my voice.

"Years ago," I said, "George Kaufman and I made a pact. If either of us ever dared address a first-night audience, the other was privileged to open fire immediately with an elephant gun. Mr. Kaufman happens to be sitting on the aisle in row B. I bid you good night."

The jubilation backstage continued for an hour.

Waiting for the newspaper reviews in the early morning editions usually keeps everyone associated with the play in suspense. Even on those occasions when a first-night audience's clamorous approval had made it patent that I'd had a hand in a hit, I was eager to read the comments of the critics.

My friend Marise Hamilton had prepared an after-theater party. When I arrived at her house at about one A.M. I intended to collect the newspapers before going home. At Marise's I found George N. Kaufman, Howard Dietz, Russel Crouse, Frank Sullivan, F.P.A., Dorothy Parker, Robert Benchley, Neysa McMean, Muriel King, the artist, Harold Ross, John Toohey, and dozens of other cronies in a state of exhilaration over my success that made it one of the happiest gatherings of my life. Shortly after I arrived we were joined by Alec Woollcott. He too was beaming. I didn't ask him what he had written. He merely ventured then, "Well, Marcus, how does it feel not to have a worry in the world?"

When the party ended about 5 A.M. I was so blissfully sleepy that I went directly home and to bed.

I did not wake until noon. Clinton, my butler-cook, brought me breakfast and his warm approval of the play. "It was fine! Really very, very fine!" he said. Learning that I was up, my mother came down from her room with a sheaf of newspaper clippings.

"How are they?" I asked. I have never forgotten the conservative statement she made as she put them beside my plate.

"For once they all understood just what you were trying to do." As I read each one I wondered if any play had pleased critics more. The briefest was that of Robert Littell in *The World*, who said that he had broken the cardinal journalistic canon that a critic must write his review on time even if he must leave the theater before the play's end. Littell said he had, without regrets, stayed until the final curtain. He promised to have a review in the next day's issue and closed his statement with words that must have delighted Rowland Stebbens' heart as much as they did mine. "In the meantime," he said, "don't let anything delay you from running to the Mansfield Theater to buy tickets."

That afternoon I did some shopping. Bobby Jones met me for lunch, after which he came with me to the Knox Hat Shop. Before rehearsals had begun, Bobby's enthusiasm over the play's prospects had led to my betting him a hat that he was wrong in his certainty of its success. In those days, the hat companies' most expensive model was the "Knox Forty." Because of its cost Bobby said he'd be happy with a less expensive headpiece. I regretted that Knox didn't have costlier lids. My next purchase was a cane for Mr. Harrison to supplant the one he used on De Lawd's visits to Earth. On its silver handle I had engraved a feeble expression of my gratitude for having the privilege of having met a truly great artist. That night, and for every performance for over four years, he never failed to carry it.

Fear of clerical disapproval had vanished. The purchase of every seat by charitable organizations for benefit performances was almost as common in 1930 as it is today. On the morning following the premiere, the first benefit performance was purchased by the Cardinal Newman Fund. For several weeks the religious columns in newspapers announcing the subject of Sunday sermons mentioned *The Green Pastures* as many as twenty times.

By now Mr. Harrison was paying the price of being a celebrity. He was eager to do anything asked of him that would promote the play, but William Fields, the head of our press department, persuaded him to except no invitations for speeches or personal appearances. Had Mr. Harrison followed his own impulses and accepted even a fraction of the invitations that swamped Fields's office he would have been a physical wreck within a week. Constant efforts were required to see that obligatory newspaper and magazine interviews did not tax Mr. Harrison's strength. As he did not leave the theater between performances on matinee days, Fields channeled most of Mr. Harrison's talks with the press into half-hour periods immediately following the afternoon performances so that the new star could get an hour of complete rest before his dinner was brought in to him. One such afternoon Wilella

Waldorf, a feature writer on the *Evening Post,* was waiting until the usual bevy of post-performance visitors to
Mr. Harrison's dressing room had left. A group of erstwhile cherubs came from their dressing rooms clad in their
street clothes on their way to their own evening meals.
Wilella saw the possibility of a good story in a juvenile
opinion of *The Green Pastures.* She stopped Miss Ruby
Davis, age eight.

"What do you think of the play, Ruby?"

"Some of it's crazy."

"Crazy?"

"Yes, ma'am. It's not true. The part about heaven is a
lie."

Wilella pressed Ruby for details.

"Well, you take the fish fry. That isn't what a fish
fry would be in heaven. In the play all the angels get to
eat are catfish and jelly sandwiches and what's suppose to
be custard. Real angels would have everything they
wanted. Strawberry shortcake, pie, chocolate sundaes, ice
cream sodas, lemonade, root beer, Coca-Cola—everything a person would want."

"What else is wrong?"

"God's office. Just an old desk and some kitchen
chairs. God would have the very finest of everything—a
gold telephone and easy chairs and lace curtains and type-
writing machine and everything like that."

Ruby's outraged disapproval went into one of the
best stories Wilella ever wrote.

Joe Byrd's brief acting career, limited to his appearances in *The Green Pastures,* was brilliant. He never failed
to enchant his audiences.

Being three years old, Joe was the youngest of the

cast. He created the role of Randolph, one of the children in the Sunday school scene. Randolph had been brought to class by his older sister and told to sit quietly beside her, a feat beyond his power. He was admiring the structure of his chair when a little ball he had been playing with slipped from his hands and rolled to the feet of Mr. Deshee, the teacher. Randolph retrieved it at the moment Mr. Deshee was trying with difficulty to convince his pupils that there was no city called New Orleans in the first moments of Creation. Never having had a close look at Mr. Deshee, Randolph gazed up admiringly at his towering figure. Gentle Charles E. Wood, who played Mr. Deshee, always managed to keep from laughing when he looked down at Joe's friendly upturned face. His part called for him to do a bit of scolding.

"Now, Randolph! If you don't listen, how you 'spect to grow up and be a good man? You wanter grow up and be a transgressor?"

Joe, living the role of Randolph, would hear the word *transgressor* for the first time and yell as loudly as he could: "No!" and everyone watching would want to hug him to death. Later in the play when Mr. Harrison as the Lord was walking the earth, Joe's was one of the three baby voices that piped, "We O.K., Lawd!" when the Lord asked, "How you little flowers makin' out?"

Joe was as popular in private life as he was with his audiences. One day his mother, who also acted in the play, did not bring him to the theater. She said he wasn't feeling well. He missed several more performances before it was learned that he had contracted tuberculosis. Joe's doctor said he might survive if he were sent to a sanatorium in the Adirondacks. His mother was shaken when told how much his treatment would cost. There was a rush of Joe's friends eager to be of help. The stagehands moved fastest. Until two years later when Joe gave up his brave fight for life, providing his material needs was the exclusive privilege of a handful of members of Local No. 1, International Alliance of Theatrical and Stage Employees.

Second only to Mr. Harrison's was the success made by Wesley Hill as Gabriel. Unlike Mr. Harrison's gentle, reserved personality, Wesley's was that of a jovial extrovert, always available for social activity. He had many friends who admired and respected him, but he was also the prey of cadging acquaintances.

Every week most of his salary went for entertainment. One day Mr. Harrison, accompanied by Alonzo Fenderson, Tutt Whitney, and other elderly and highly respected members of the cast had a long and earnest talk with the too-amiable Wesley and his distressed wife. As a result Wesley's salary was turned over each week to Mr. Harrison. He and his fellow committeemen allotted Wesley a reasonable amount of spending money, gave Mrs. Hill what she needed for her household expenses, and put the rest in a bank account, unavailable even to Mrs. Hill, whose affection for Wesley would have resulted in her giving him anything he asked for. His monetary discipline did not handicap Wesley's social life, but, from then on, his pleasant times were spent with people who deserved his friendship. One afternoon about a year later Wesley was crossing a Harlem street when a speeding truck killed him. Three thousand mourners attended his funeral.

When his estate was settled *The Green Pastures* trusteeship was able to turn over a small fortune to his widow.

In April the play had settled down for a long run

with advance sales extending into September and October. The theaters of New York had not yet begun to be air-conditioned, but a slight alleviation of the summer heat was prepared for by the thoughtful Bill Fields. There was a moment in the play when De Lawd found the sunlight in Heaven a little too warm for comfort. His brief command for an improvement was printed on thousands of paper fans to be furnished to summer theatergoers. "Let it be jest a little bit cooler."

Charles Cochran, outstanding among British play producers, was eager to put on *The Green Pastures* in London. In May I sailed for England to discuss arrangements. I had met him on several previous visits and had found him, like his many friends, warm and engaging and a brilliant showman. We had several pleasant meetings, during which ways and means were discussed preliminary to our signing a contract. One day we were having lunch when one of the Cochran staff hurried to our table in the Savoy Grill with a shocking bulletin. The Lord Chamberlain had a half-hour before banned the production of *The Green Pastures* in any British theater. Cochran was as stunned as I. In our discussions, the question of the play's possible conflict with the rule forbidding the presence of the Deity on a stage had been anticipated. Cochran had been certain that he could convince the Lord Chamberlain's office that there was no irreverence in my play and that the unanimous clerical embracement in the United States demonstrated its religious appeal. Cochran rushed to a telephone. He returned with the news that, completely without authority to do so, another London manager, ignorant of my negotiation with Cochran, had submitted the play for approval before he himself made a bid for the production rights. Cochran was told by the Lord Chamberlain himself that he had not read the play, that it had been turned down automatically by a subordinate, but that protocol obliged him to support the decision.

Because of its phenomenal reception in America, *The Green Pastures* was well known to Britishers. *The Evening Standard* had bought rights to publish it serially. All the London papers made headlines of the banning, and within a few days the privileges of British censorship were challenged by angry partisans. Bernard Shaw, H. G. Wells, and other writers wrote blazing letters to *The Times* and other journals. Lady Astor raised cain in Parliament. It was reported that King George had privately expressed his dislike of the order, and the Archbishop of York headed members of the cloth who felt the banning was absurd. The hasty and uninvited action had ruined any chance of the play's production in England.

Its banning there was, oddly enough, helpful to American producers and authors. When I returned to New York at the end of the summer, a bill was introduced in Congress providing for a federal censorship. When delegates from the Dramatists' Guild and other writers' organizations appeared in Washington at the bill's hearings, their testimony on the fate of my play in England resulted in the bill's quick demise. To this day, *Pastures*, while produced privately by schools, has never been seen publicly in England. Because the Lord Chamberlain's office has no control over motion pictures, the licenses for movies are granted by the London County Counsel, and the film version of the play was shown throughout the British Isles without protest except by fundamentalists in Scotland who had neither read nor seen the play. A few years ago I prepared a script of the play for the BBC—also out of the Lord Chamberlain's domain—which was telecast without intermission and received cordially.

Other parts of Europe were not so hypersensitive to the play. In 1932 I made a stormy December crossing in the old Gripsholm for its first continental production. Erik Wettergren, the director of Dramaten, the Swedish state theater in Stockholm, had faced a problem in translating the play's Deep South dialect of the American Negro into something like a Swedish folk speech. It was solved by a Finnish scholar, who used the Swedish dialect of Dalacarlia, a province in central Sweden whose inhabitants are noted for their quaint speech and adherence to ancient dress and folkways. A gentle giant of an actor named Georg Blickenberg played De Lawd with beautiful simplicity and strength. There were no Negro actors in Sweden, so the white cast played in minstrel makeup. Olov Molander's direction was superb, and because of the dimensions of the Dramaten stage he was able to achieve stage effects impossible at the Mansfield, whose stage depth was only half that of the Dramaten. A turntable forty-five feet in diameter allowed heavy sets to be placed back to back so that scenes could be changed even more swiftly than they were in New York.

The play had been running for several weeks when I came to see it. Its success was immediate. The Dramaten, traditionally a repertory theater, presented it two-hundred times before two duplicate productions of *Guds Grönna Ängar* were organized to tour the rest of Sweden.

I learned that a minor but unhappy incident had marred the first performance. Despite the presence of royalty inside, a gang of rowdies had severely beaten a theater-carriage starter named Max Taylor who had been engaged, Mr. Wettergren told me, because he was a Negro. The next afternoon I went to visit him in the hospital where he was recuperating. He had virtually recovered from his beating and was about to be sent home. He told me he was an American, but his speech was unlike any I had ever heard in the United States. I asked him where he had been born. Self-consciously he asked if he could speak to me alone, and Arvid Englund, my Swedish agent, who had been guiding me about the city, left us together. "Max Taylor" then unburdened himself of a guilty secret. He said he was a boxer and had fought in St. Louis and other towns, but that he had told the theater manager he was an American Negro only to get the job. His natural complexion was reasonably dark, and he had not felt it necessary to say his mother had been a Filipino and his father a Swedish sailor.

February 26, 1930, is a date I shall never forget because it marked the premiere of *The Green Pastures*. May 30th of the same year also left itself indelibly on my mind because of another unusual experience. I shared it with a small boy. In retrospect I think we both felt it approached the miraculous.

Mende is in the south of France in the department of Lozère, and I was in Mende because, despite the approach of summer, there was snow on the road leading north to Paris. I had to wait in Mende until the road was clear.

The anniversary of the martyrdom of Joan of Arc was a holiday. The schools were closed, and the town fathers had prepared a day-long program of athletic events. The pupils of Mende's primary schools would supply the forenoon activities. Among the scheduled diver-

sions was "Un Ballet Indien," to be followed by a basketball game, the first ever played in public by Mende's
school children.

I strolled about the town square, waiting for the
action to begin. As I looked about me I wondered if the
arrangements committee had ever seen basketball played
anywhere. The hoops seemed to be fixed at regulation
height on poles properly distanced, but the game promised
to be a noteworthy variation from orthodox contests. It
would be interesting to discover how the players were going to dribble the ball and avoid bruising collisions on a
playing surface of lumpy cobblestones.

A whistle announced the start of "Un Ballet Indien."
About fifty boys ranging in age from eight to ten stood in
two long lines facing each other. They were similarly
dressed in cotton jackets and trousers meant to represent
buckskin suits. Paper fringes substituted for strips of
leather. Their war bonnets were obviously homemade, but
at least in silhouette suggested a gathering of chieftains. In
each small right hand was a wooden tomahawk. For defense every left arm held a knight's shield reduced in scale
but in shape not unlike those carried at Crécy and Agin-
court. As their designers were unfamiliar with American
Indian heraldry, the shields were all uniformly emblazoned
with lions rampant.

A tall, stern figure whose long black coat and stiff
black hat suggested that in private life he might be an un-
dertaker stood at the foot of the two lines. After a dramatic pause he began counting off movements for the
dancers. They were quite simple. As he barked *"Un!"* the
right feet of one line went forward. Simultaneously its
right arms lifted the tomahawks aggressively. The opposite

line stepped back and raised its shields. At *"Deux!"* the lines resumed their original positions. *"Trois!"* reversed the pressures of battle, the original attackers now on the defensive. *"Quatre!"* and all were again at rest.

The same movements were repeated over and over to the conductor's monotonous *"Un! Deux! Trois! Quatre!"* I gave up hoping for any variance and was considering moving away when a sound resembling a faint sob drew my attention to a small figure beside me. He was, I should say, about eleven. Alone among the spectators he was taking no interest in the ballet. His costume indicated that he was on one of the basketball teams. He wore a white cotton T-shirt and gym trunks of a material seldom used in sports apparel, shiny glazed chintz. In the ballet's audience were other costumes like his, differing only in that the trunks of one team were mauve, the other's bright orange. My neighbor was on the orange team.

At first I attributed his quiet sobs and slight shivering to the coldness of the air and the thinness of his costume. He must have sensed my looking at him for his eyes lifted to mine and communicated an unqualified wretchedness behind them. They were not tearful. Their owner had not yet reached the point of discomfort when tears could not be repressed.

"Un! Deux! Trois! Quatre!" the dour drill master shouted, his voice growing louder as the end of the dreary war dance approached. I looked down again at my companion. This time his eyes were waiting for mine. The face that had been filled with misery was now racked by anguish, anguish caused by something other than the chilling air. As I watched him, the incessant counting ended and the weary braves stopped threatening each other. There

was applause. Someone announced that as soon as the ballet's audience withdrew to the sides of the square the basketball game would get underway. The audience started to thin. The unhappy boy beside me did not budge. Now tears were streaming down his cheeks. His look had turned into an expression of unutterable despair. There was no plea for help in his agonized young face nor an unvoiced bid for sympathy from the stranger watching him. Only mute despondency as he waited for some imminent, agonizing inevitability.

It was impossible for me to move away. I put my arm around his shoulder and urged him to tell me the nature of his crisis. He looked wildly about and then with a sob that would have broken God's heart he pointed to his trunks. In less than a minute he would be called to the center of the square and the whole town of Mende would see the stain that had darkened the orange brilliance of the glazed chintz.

If ever there was a proper moment for a miracle it was then. The voice of the master of ceremonies blared. *"Messieurs et mesdames. Maintenant le premier jeu de basketball dans l'histoire du Mende sera—"* He stopped abruptly. People began moving hurriedly away from the plaza.

I looked at the small boy. He was gazing at me now incandescent with wonder and relief. All his problems were gone. He smiled and I smiled back at him. Then we both rushed to cover as the rain came down more heavily.

The first royal personage I ever met was the present King Gustav. He was a guest of San Francisco's Bohemian

Club at its annual fortnight of frolic in Bohemian Grove, the club's immense forest retreat. Among the entertainment there was the annual spectacular performance in the grove's enormous outdoor theater. An orchestra of two-hundred musicians seated before a proscenium framed by two towering redwoods, accompanied the playing of poet George Sterling's impressive allegorical verse-drama, *Truth*. In the final scene, the heroine Truth stood naked and alone on a natural elevation hundreds of feet above rising stage levels on which hundreds of actors representing blind humanity were worshiping the bits of clothing she had shed in escaping hypocrisy and deceit.

In Stockholm I met Gustav's two great-uncles, the princes Eugene and William, younger brothers of the late tennis-loving King Gustaf V. The Bernadotte line of Swedish royalty has been rich with scholars and artists. King Gustav is a distinguished archaeologist. Prince Eugene was a talented painter whose royal status prevented the commercial disposal of fine oils and drawings that hang in many of the world's great museums. Prince William was a gifted historian. His highly regarded books and treatises are still widely read. I frequently visited Prince Eugene in his charming studio-residence in Stockholm harbor. Prince William and I formed a friendship that lasted until his death in 1965. It began with a merry argument in the automatic elevator of the residence of the American Minister. I did not recognize the tall, slender man who smiled at me as I pressed the button that would take me to the upper floor where the Minister was giving a cocktail party reception in my honor. Photographs of me had appeared many times in the Stockholm papers, so I was not startled when the smiling man beside me asked if I was Mr. Connelly and identified himself as Prince William. He too was going to the reception, and when the elevator stopped and the door opened automatically at the apartment, he politely indicated that I should leave first. I knew nothing of elevator protocol, but I said, "After your Royal Highness."

"Oh, no!" said Prince William. "You are a guest of my country and you must let me be hospitable."

With mock gravity: "Sir, at the moment we are standing on what is by international law American territory, so you are a guest of the United States." I swept my hand toward the open door. Prince William did not give up. "You have made an error," he said. "The floor a foot ahead of us may be technically the United States, but we are standing in a Swedish lift directly above Swedish ground."

At that moment our hostess appeared, to see us backed against opposite walls of the elevator, our arms folded, regarding each other with what looked like stern defiance. She stared at us nonplused and then ventured uncertainly, "Good afternoon, Prince William."

Before she could say more, Prince William, poker-faced, said, "Madame, I am having difficulty getting one of your fellow countrymen to leave Sweden."

I put in my oar: "I have been only trying to extend hospitality to a royal visitor on American soil. Do you realize, sir, that the breach we are facing may lead to war." Prince William saw that our hostess would be puzzled even more if the clowning was continued. We both laughed, and the poor woman got the point.

"War must be avoided at any cost," she said.

"Then you solve the problem," said Prince William.

"In a crisis like this I will rely on American statesmanship."

"I think you're both a bit mad, so you will march out of this elevator shoulder to shoulder."

In my subsequent visits to Sweden I had many more happy encounters with Prince William. In 1951 we were together for the last time when I flew from Oslo at the conclusion of an International Theatre Institute congress to attend the sixtieth birthday festivities of my friend Carl Gustav Bjorkman, the writer-publisher who was also the drama critic of the *Dagens Nyheter*. When any distinguished Swede reaches fifty and sixty his birthday is recognized by an old national custom. He is privately offered congratulations and usually is the guest of honor at family dinners, but unless he places an advertisement in the newspapers requesting its omission a great subscription banquet is organized to acknowledge his importance to the community. Such occasions are formal, white-tie affairs with the women guests wearing décolletage and long opera gloves. Carl Gustav's public dinner was an unusually gallant occasion, and the supper dance that followed it was held at Stockholm's great Bellmans Ro Restaurant. My knowledge of Swedish is fragmentary, but from the hilarity about me it was quite evident that Prince William was being a suave and witty toastmaster. When the speeches had ended and the dancing had begun, Prince William joined the group at the table where Carl Gustav and I were seated. With his usual warm concern, he asked if I was enjoying my first Swedish birthday party.

"Greatly," I said. "It's been a novel experience in more

ways than one. I have known you for more than twenty-five years but I never heard you speak Swedish until to-night." The same solemn look I had first encountered in an elevator was turned on.

"It may have been unfamiliar to you," he said gravely, "but I promise you, I speak it like a native."

On my first visit to Stockholm, Prince William introduced me to Dr. Agne Beijer who, a few years earlier, had made himself famous by a discovery as important to theater lovers as Schliemann's unearthing of Troy was to archaeologists. A graduate student of the University of Stockholm, the twenty-six-year-old Beijer wanted to submit a doctoral dissertation on Sweden's Royal Theater at Drottningholm, a small island fifteen minutes by car from Stockholm. In the mid-eighteenth century it had been the summer retreat of the ruling family. In the 1780s, a handsome theater had been built on the palace grounds by the father of Gustav III, who had written and acted in many of its productions and had instilled in his son his own love for the stage. Under Gustav III, playwrights, composers, actors, choreographers, play directors, and scene designers throughout Europe vied for invitations to the Royal Theater at Drottningholm. Bellman, the Swedish Heine, was the court dramatist. Several of his plays and operas came to life at Drottningholm.

Gustav's cultural activities were part of his program for strengthening his country's nationalism. Many Russians were disturbed by Sweden's growing strength, and one night at a costume ball an assassin, disguised as a guest, plunged a dagger into Gustav's heart. The bloodstained cloak he was wearing can be seen in the National Museum, but a more widely known memento of the killing is Verdi's opera "Un Ballo in Maschera" which perpetuates it. The next day the doors of the theater closed, its activities ended.

The young student Beijer came to Drottningholm to do firsthand research on his thesis. His efforts to study the theater itself were thwarted by the avowal of palace custodians that the theater had long ceased to exist. None could tell him when it had been torn down. One or two vaguely recalled that it had been destroyed by fire.

"There has certainly never been a fire," he contended. "All the palace buildings are of wood and so clustered that had there been a blaze of any size the meager equipment for fighting it could not have stopped its spread to the other structures." His persistence gained him authority to enter a building that had been closed for many decades. When its doors were opened, out fell some of the jammed clutter within, but when a passage was made through it, Beijer found that the congestion extended only to other doorways. Furniture and rubbish discarded over the years had filled only the lobby of Gustav's playhouse. Beyond it, abandoned and almost untouched by dust and decay, lay the original ingeniously contrived auditorium. A royal box, the upholstery of its chairs untarnished by age, faced a smaller one, which apparently had been reserved for the royal barber.

Backstage, Beijer came upon a treasure of undamaged scenery and other stage equipment. Small cannonballs lay at the end of a sliding trough in which they had made stage thunder. There were long foot-thick cylinders surfaced like Byzantine columns for rolling lengthwise so that the cloth above them could simulate ocean waves, and slots through which scenery could be raised and lowered by still usable windlasses. The theater's storerooms revealed hundreds of costumes for contemporary eighteenth century plays and those of earlier periods. On a dressing-room mirror was an amateurish greasepaint caricature by one of the actors who had last seen himself reflected there.

Agne Beijer's discovery resulted in his being made the theater's curator. Under his devoted care it became the foremost theatrical museum in the world. Annual performances were given of old plays exactly as they had been seen by their first audiences, the only material difference in their production being small electric lights of the same power as the original candles. The new lights were strengthened by the original reflectors behind them.

When Adlai Stevenson was preparing to visit Sweden in 1958, I wrote Agne Beijer, who now wore the title of Professor, the highest academic honor Sweden affords, and asked if he would show Stevenson his Drottningholm treasures. He not only served as guide to the Stevenson party but arranged a special performance of an *opera bouffe* that Bellman had written to celebrate one of his king's birthdays.

Before my first trip to Sweden something I said about radio in a newspaper interview, led to several conversations with Henry Ford. In the interview I had argued that radio advertisers should recognize, as playwrights had done for centuries, that suggestion was always a better device than statement across the footlights. I felt that while blatant claims familiarized listeners with a product's name, they antagonized more people than they persuaded. I argued that superior entertainment rather than crafty commercials would benefit sponsors more.

Mr. Ford was reluctant to begin radio advertising until he found the kind of program that satisfied him. It was thought that I might help him come to a deicision. The several trips I made to Michigan gave me many private glimpses of the creator of the biggest industrial monolith in history.

On my first visit to his headquarters in Dearborn I encountered Mr. Ford's scale of values before we actually met. A frieze of names carved above the entrance of the engineering building was a list of the men who Mr. Ford believed had made major contributions to man's wellbeing. They were great names, but each was related to material accomplishments. Only one represented the humanities. Da Vinci was there because of the esteem Mr. Ford had for him as an engineer.

Mr. Ford could not have been more hospitable in welcoming me and taking me on tours of his vast domain. He must have been told I was a playwright, but in all our conversations he always called me professor. Our first lunch together was shared with his son Edsel, his close friend, W. J. Cameron, the editor of the Dearborn *Independent*, and other lieutenant-executives of his company. More than a dozen of us sat at a round table, the center of which was an enormous basket of carrots, celery, and other raw vegetables. My host answered ingenuous questions about the beginnings and prewar development of his business interests. He told me graphically and with curious simplicity of unproductive negotiations with Czarist Russia for farm equipment. The identity of a negotiator slipped his memory. He turned to his son.

"Edsel, what was the name of that Grand Duke who wanted all those tractors on trust?"

A few minutes later I was learning about the great plant being erected in Japan for making Ford cars when the tooting of a locomotive on the nearby Michigan Central tracks halted him. He consulted his watch, then glanced at our companions.

"You fellows got 12:06?" Most of the other watches read so. "It's either an extra section on number three or the 12:10 is early again."

It was on that first visit that I was shown the as-yet-uncompleted Greenfield Village, that amazingly inclusive museum of physical history. Under the same roof, every kind of bicycle ridden for a century and a half and a myriad of other antiquated evidences of past ingenuity were being catalogued for display.

Greenfield Village had been named for Mr. Ford's birthplace, a nearby farming community. I found many of the museum units already completed. Everything in Greenfield Village had to work. There was an early American grist mill with a functioning conveyor belt.

"That's where I got the idea for the automobile assembly line," said Mr. Ford.

The most inclusive echo of earlier days was an 1850 American general store that I recalled greatly to my advantage a few years later. The stock of goods in the store included contemporary men's and women's clothing, piles of unsold suits and dresses from old storehouses. The haberdashery included unworn paper collars and cuffs, shoes, suspenders, hats and undershirts and drawers suitable for arctic wear. A circle of sturdy chairs surrounded a serviceable potbellied stove, and small, conveniently placed sawdust-filled boxes on the floor were ready for the use of purchasers of the aged tobacco on display beside boxes of now rather dry cigars. The mouth of a child of today would have watered at the jars filled with candies and licorice strips. His mother might have been tempted by some of the coffee, tea, and other staples or found a desirable saucepan among the kitchenware.

When I was preparing the production of *The Farmer Takes a Wife* I wanted to create as faithfully as I could the atmosphere of the Erie Canal in the early 1850s. The audiences never realized that the kerosene can in the canalside hotel was authentic or that the wallpaper was identical in appearance with a fragment Donald Oenslager had found decorating the abandoned office of a long-dead locktender of the Five Combines below Rome, New York. Don, Walter Edmonds, from whose *Rome Haul* the play had been adapted, and I spend a fortnight doing research along the old canal route. *The Farmer* had a scene in the galley of a typical freight boat of the period.

I wrote Mr. Ford that in the loft of the general store in Greenfield Village I had seen an as-yet-unpacked case containing several dozen rolling pins that had been made for use in 1850 kitchens. They were made of glass and filled with baking soda, which could be emptied by unscrewing a metal cap on one of the handles. The empty pin could then be filled with cold water, which was believed to improve the texture of the pastry rolled under it. I asked if I might borrow one of them to use as a prop. A week later a wooden case, more an example of cabinet-making than carpentry, arrived from Dearborn. Within it, nestling in velvet concavities, were two of the rolling pins.

In one of our early talks, Mr. Ford said that if he *did* go in for radio advertising he knew the music he was going to use. It would be the Seth Parker singers, who specialized in fundamentalist hymns. He was tolerant, however, to my suggestion that other forms of music might help the prestige of Ford cars. I said that a poll had shown that among the fifty thousand employees in his River Rouge plant, there were musicians representing a dozen national cultures. A potpourri of the classical music of the different countries was arranged and recorded. Eventually Mr. Ford's entry into radio advertising was by way of orchestral concerts. Halfway through each program, W. J. Cameron gave paternal homilies that Mr. Ford considered highly important morally.

Although Greenfield Village was not yet open to the public, visitors were welcome to drive about in horse-drawn vehicles, from calabash to opera coach. The only motor car permitted was the one Mr. Ford chose for his own transport. On my last day in Dearborn, he invited me to ride with him to hear the music of the organ just installed in the newly completed Greenfield Village chapel, named the Chapel of Mary and Martha, in honor of his mother and an aunt. It was a warm spring day, and as we approached the chapel my host stopped the car so that we could hear from a distance the strains of "Pomp and Circumstance" being played by the newly installed organist. After listening for a minute, Mr. Ford suggested that we say hello to the organist. He released the car's brakes and attempted to start the ignition. The engine did not respond. He pulled this, turned that, pressed knobs and pedals. The car failed to start. He shook his head and looked at me.

"They are always changing the damn things!" he said with a sigh.

Martinez Sierra's *Cradle Song* is a lovely play, the gentle, poignant story of Sister Joanna, a Spanish novice nun who becomes the foster mother of a baby girl left at the convent's door. The narrative deals movingly with Joanna's maternal love as the foundling grows to womanhood and finally marries.

"The situation is entirely changed," urged the agent. "Now a playwright has an incentive to work for something besides money. The talkies depend on dialogue, not captions. Paramount wants you to make a film version of *The Cradle Song*."

I set out again for Hollywood, I wrote the script, guided through the unfamiliar technical requirements by the talented and sensitive Frank Partos. I was in New York when Frank saw the completed picture at the studio.

He wrote, "It will remind you in several places of our script. Someone decided to make a change in Joanna's family background. If I described it you wouldn't believe me."

I saw the picture a few weeks later. In casting it, the producer had had a typical Hollywood inspiration. The actress he selected as ideal for the part of Joanna was one who had very effectively portrayed a sinister instructress in the highly successful German picture *Maedchen in Uni-*

form. To justify her broken English the producer inserted a scene in which it was explained that when three years old, Joanna had been the only survivor of a shipwreck in which her German parents had drowned. One was not told why fifteen years later she still spoke with a heavy German accent.

My next visit to Hollywood had happier results. Irving Thalberg, the production chief of Metro-Goldwyn-Mayer, invited me to adapt Kipling's *Captains Courageous.* Thalberg was the embodiment of the self-deluding influences of the world of the movies. He worked fourteen hours a day on the M.G.M. lot, completely insulated from the nonmovie world. At night he went home to a Santa Monica beach mansion that was air-conditioned to exclude the tangy smell of the ocean and sound-proofed so that he would not hear the roar of the surf.

Working on *Captains Courageous* was the most satisfying experience I was to have in Hollywood. Louis Leighton, its producer, was being ostracized by the studio hierarchy because he wouldn't play office politics. Gossip had it that *Captains Courageous* would be his last picture at M.G.M. The director was to be Victor Fleming, also in general disfavor, owing to his contempt for the jackal practices he frequently encountered in the studio world. Because of his outspoken disdain for several officials, he had the status of a pariah, which he was quite content to accept. I am sure the privacy enjoyed by Fleming and Leighton during the picture's preparation was a major factor in its becoming one of the studio's greatest successes. Subsequently, Leighton was offered better contracts than he had ever enjoyed. Fleming's already secure prestige was enhanced. His next directorial assignment was *Gone With the Wind*.

The early thirties at M.G.M. were marked by the importation of authors from every field of writing. Those who proved inept as "constructionists" or dialogue writers did not stay long, but it was said that if anyone could sign his name to a contract he was sure of an annual salary of at least $100,000—for two weeks. Those who were retained were men and women who brought proven talents with them. P. G. Wodehouse was able to write several Jeeves stories while waiting, on salary, almost a year for a studio assignment. Writers noted for their individual creativity were dazed by the material on which they were told to work. Dorothy Parker's biting wit and unsentimental compassion were considered by one producer as ideal assets for adapting that early wave of a flood of soap operas, *Madame X*.

William Faulkner's advent at M.G.M. made an impression long remembered. We had been friends since 1929, when he came to New York for the publication of *The Sound and the Fury*. His speech was always slow, partly because of his natural southern drawl and partly because of a conversational gambit he habitually employed. Before answering a question he would exhale a long, meditative puff from his straight-stemmed pipe; then, as often as not, he would contemplate the bowl for a few seconds more.

When he first met Thalberg, Bill was asked if he was familiar with M.G.M. productions. "Ah don't believe Ah know which pictures are yours," Bill replied. "Do you make the Mickey Mouse brand?"

"No," Thalberg replied icily, "we make some shorts, but we want you to familiarize yourself with our big features and the work of our leading stars."

Bill said he'd be happy to do so. A projection room was placed at his disposal where he could privately enjoy the latest masterpieces of Lana Turner and Norma Shearer. Actually he *was* ignorant of the work of both. Ten minutes after Bill entered the projection room he dashed out, almost colliding with another writer. The anguish on Faulkner's face made the latter ask:

"What's the matter?"

For once, Bill did not puff on his pipe before pronouncing his impression of M.G.M. epics:

"Jesus Christ, it ain't possible!"

Bill had rented a small flat on Santa Monica Boulevard from which he came daily to his office in the studio.

"You needn't come here every day just to write, you know," said his producer. "If you'd rather work at home, feel free to do so."

So Faulkner promptly went back to Oxford, Mississippi.

Lunchtime usually saw the writers' table in the M.G.M. commissary crowded. Payment for the whole table bill was determined by casting dice. The lowest number thrown determined who would be host. One day Herman Mankiewicz got a bright idea. For five dollars he offered to insure anyone at the table against being stuck with the check. One week Mank's legendary bad luck stayed with him four days in succession. His single client's low throws cost Mankiewicz over two hundred dollars.

Samuel Hoffenstein, press agent and versifier—you'll find a lot of pre-Ogden Nash humor in his *Poems in Praise of Practically Nothing*—and Louis Weitzenkorn, author of the highly successful play *Five Star Final*, were also frequenters of the M.G.M. writers' table. One day an unsolicited scenario for a movie was received by the M.G.M. script department. Knowing the difficulty of getting a script read except through a recognized agent, the author had attached this note:

> Don't be too hasty tossing this story into a waste basket. You will notice that its envelope is postmarked Wilkes Barre, Pennsylvania. Let me remind you that Wilkes Barre breeds writers. It gave M.G.M. Herman J. Mankiewicz, Samuel Hoffenstein, and Louis Weitzenkorn.

A few days later the informative author was sent the following:

> Thank you for your note about Wilkes Barre. We are sending back your script, which we cannot use. We are also returning Herman J. Mankiewicz, Samuel Hoffenstein, and Louis Weitzenkorn.

George Haight, a former writer, still ate with us after he became a producer. He, too, brought a business interest to the table. George's studio salary was probably at least twenty-five hundred dollars a week, but to all appearances his main interest in life was his exclusive agency rights for the products of the Ajax Novelty Company, of Paterson, New Jersey. George was forever demonstrating his goods, to the delight of the luncheon crowd. Without warning you would find yourself drinking from a dribble glass, watching a spoon melt in a coffee cup, or discovering a fly in a lump of sugar.

George also sold book matches. For two dollars he would supply you with a carton of them with your name and, if you wished, advertisement on the cover. Harry Kurnitz invested in two cartons. One read: "Scenarios neatly done." The other: "Our hands our only tools." George said he expected to net between four and seven dollars in commissions before the buying rush ended.

One day I asked him how one of his scheduled pictures was progressing.

"Not so good. I'm supposed to have a shooting script ready in four or five weeks. I don't like the story line Doc and Charlie have been working on, but I can't get them to change it."

"Then why don't you have them taken off the script and get other writers?"

The exclusive agent of the Ajax Novelty Company glared.

"No, by God! Those bastards don't get off this picture until they've given me orders for matches!"

The new building in which writers had their offices was commodious, but its walls were rather thin. Zoë Akins, author of *Déclassée* and other successful plays, although born and raised in Missouri, had a curiously affected English speech. When considering the purchase of a house she said she felt that the "prace was a bit too haigh." One day she summoned the building superintendent to her office. It was difficult to work she said because of the sound of "mace" in the wall near her desk. The superintendent investigated. In an adjoining office he found a couple of writers seated on the floor shooting craps. The wall was serving as a buffer for each throw. He returned to Zoë's office with his report.

"It's not mace, Miss Akins. It's dace."

One of the joys of being in Hollywood was the presence of so many friends from New York. As our studios were scattered about town, we frequently met for lunch at the Brown Derby in Beverly Hills. Something like the old Algonquin atmosphere attended a big corner table where half a dozen of us would gather. It was there that Benchley, Oscar Hammerstein, Charles Butterworth, Harry Ruby, Charles Lederer, myself, and one or two others began amusing ourselves by discussing plans for an imaginary annual picnic of a social club that didn't exist but called to mind similar organizations we had known in our boyhoods. Nostalgically remembered committees were appointed. One reported on the progress of negotiations with a might-have-been street-car company for transportation to and from the picnic grounds. It was pointed out that the previous year, considerable money had been saved by paying a flat rate of $1.75 per carload of passengers. Paying the 5-cent fare individually would run the cost well over $2.00.

Another committee was to write to the flour mill for baseball caps, a third to solicit local merchants for prizes for the athletic events. We had trouble deciding what nonexistent baseball team we would take on at the picnic. While this was being argued Charlie Butterworth made a proposal. The club had no official name. If we would name it after him he would contribute a catcher's mitt and mask and fielders' gloves for the other players. Our organization then became the Butterworth Athletic Club. The day following its naming, Oscar Hammerstein generously wrote two songs for the organization. One was a pep song that went as follows:

"B-U-double-T-E-R-W-O-R-T-H!
That spells many a happy day
With companions brave and gay
And when we play the Eagles
Who gets left in the lurch?
Not the B-U-double-T-E-R-W-O-R-T-Urch!"

Oscar also wrote a club hymn. I've forgotten all but the impressive opening lines:

Butterworth, Oh Butterworth,
Thy name shall be for aye . . .

Oscar's wife Dorothy, on learning of the club's existence, formed a Ladies Auxiliary. My impression is that Dorothy was the Auxiliary's only member. However, the distaff side of the B.A.C. presented each of the male members with a terrycloth scarf handsomely embroidered with the club's monogram.

For weeks our lunchtime gatherings were brightened by such nonsense. One day work kept me at the studio at lunchtime. In the late afternoon I drove to Oscar Hammerstein's house at the top of La Brea for our almost-daily badminton game. I asked if he had attended that day's meeting at the Brown Derby.

"I did," he said.

"What happened?"

Before replying, he added a point to his score by

neatly dropping a shuttlecock just over the net and out of my reach.

"I resigned."

"I can't believe it. What happened?"

The game halted as he sadly explained.

"You know how hard I've worked for the club, writing the pep song, the hymn and all. Well, today it dawned on me that I've never been put on one God-damned committee!"

It was characteristic of Charlie Butterworth to cancel his California engagements and come to New York immediately when I asked him to take part in a benefit I was organizing for the Authors' League and Stage Relief Funds. We called it the *Depression Gaieties* and presented it at the Imperial Theater.

While Phil Baker, the Sixty-Four-Dollar Question man, was giving an accordion solo, Charlie crossed the stage with a step ladder, by which he climbed into a box. From there he heckled Baker and had the audience in stitches. Everyone else I asked to participate in the show also responded. Richard Rodgers, Larry Hart, George and Ira Gershwin, Oscar Hammerstein, Arthur Schwartz, Howard Dietz, Jerome Kern, and George M. Cohan wrote original songs, some of which were sung with Paul Whiteman's band.

Noel Coward wrote a skit called *Design for Rehearsal*, in which Lynn Fontanne, Alfred Lunt, and he made hilarious fun of their rehearsals of *Design for Living*. Beatrice Lillie and Fanny Brice introduced most of the acts by coming on in tights and reciting doggerel in the manner of the lisping chorus girls George White used in his revues:

> And now we vow
> Whatcha gonna see will be a wow.

A little later they droned:

> And now if you will kindly lithen
> We'll let you see the next act. Thith'n.

In one sketch Bea was the mistress of a children's sedate dancing school. Her little pupils included Fred and Adele Astaire, Buddy Ebsen, who then was the dancing partner of his sister Vilma, Clifton Webb, Claire Luce, and others.

Another novelty was the appearance of four composers whose names may not be easily recalled today but who, as F.P.A. said in introducing them, had written songs that glow in America's social history. Harry von Tilzer sang his "Wait Till the Sun Shines, Nelly." Harry Armstrong was still musically vocal with his legacy to all barbershop quartets, "Sweet Adeline." W. C. Handy rendered his "St. Louis Blues," and finally Charles Metz conducted Bill Daly's orchestra as they played "There'll Be a Hot Time in the Old Town Tonight," which he wrote in 1896. He said he'd never heard it played by an orchestra before. Some of his contemporaries recalled it had been played on trumpets when it carried Theodore Roosevelt's Rough Riders up San Juan Hill.

A dozen skits were written for the occasion as vehicles for Willie Howard, Bobby Clark, Judith Anderson, Victor Moore, Constance Collier, Madge Kennedy, Fred

Allen, Hope Williams, Hugh O'Connell, Charles Winninger, Jack Pearl, Bill Robinson, Imogene Coca, Clifton
Webb, Ethel Merman, Jimmy Savo, Rudy Vallee, Ethel
Barrymore, and several more stage artists, who are now
forgotten. Escudero and his Spanish troupe topped off the
dancing contributions.

Benchley was present too. As a visiting English novelist he evoked audience hysteria in a now forgotten monologue, "How I Create." In telling how he wrote his exquisite prose he found it difficult to address simultaneously
his listeners out front and the electrician who came on
stage to extricate him from some electric cables in which
his feet had become entangled.

Dorothy Parker and Frank Sullivan collaborated on
the printed program. Frank wrote a history of benefit performances. Part of it read:

> The earliest known record of an actual Benefit Per-
> formance is contained in an inscription on an old piece
> of toast discovered in the alley behind the Astor in 1923.
> It describes a benefit staged for Hammurabi, King of
> Babylonia, circa 2180 B.C., by one Dan Froh Man, who
> later became the Uncle Daniel Frohman who has played
> such an important part in the development of the Benefit
> throughout the ages.
>
> Let us not go into the Benefit Performance as it was
> known to the Greeks because Greek is very difficult for
> me and dislocates my jaw. Let us, rather, pass to a survey
> of the miracle play Benefits of mediaeval times. The pro-
> ceeds were always donated to the Church, hence it was
> known as the Benefit of Clergy. There you go again,
> George.
>
> Space and the fact that the writer's beard is hope-
> lessly entangled in the typewriter, forbids a detailed dis-
> cussion of the Benefit Performances of modern times.

One must, however, recall the one given by Sir Harry Lauder for Andrew Carnegie early in the century. Carnegie had speculated heavily in libraries and had lost his fortune. The Benefit which Sir Harry (and Daniel Frohman) staged for him, however, netted $235,000,000 and enabled the old financier to spend the rest of his days free from financial worry.

The future of the Benefit Performance? Ah, how hard it is to predict, in these parlous times. Dare we hope that some day, if civilization has not in the meantime tottered and fallen, some Great Leader will arise who will invent a Benefit for the Benefit of Actors who have played at Benefits for the Benefit of Others?

Dotty's contribution to the program was a variety of advertisements. One read:

COMPLIMENTS OF A FOE

Another:

Couple leaving Washington early in March to spend remainder of winter in Palo Alto, California, will exchange fifty used electoral votes for lift in automobile headed toward coast. Apply H. H., General Delivery, Washington, D.C.

There was the ad of Sisson, Misson, Bisson, Kisson, Doop & Sweedle, a real-estate firm:

We have a number of select benches available for rental in several of the city's most exclusive parks. Completely equipped with old newspapers, fountains with running water and modern conveniences. Our motto: All the Comforts of a Comfort Station. No lease, no references, no beer, no work.

There was another, the copy of which ran:

STRAWSON & MAWSON, Printers, Paperhangers and Paperhangers. "Have you tried our new Depression wall paper? It consists of only the very best selected quality of Krueger and Toll shares, in attractive pastel shades, done in a variety of smart, modern designs. If you have a roof over your head, let us paper it."

Two years later, because many authors and actors were still hungry, we cooked up another benefit, *The Post-Depression Gaieties*, which was given in the New Amsterdam Theater. Besides many of those in the earlier show, we had Jack Benny. For the first time he did his droll "interview" with a trio of girl applicants for his radio show.

Most New York drama critics were in a western melodrama called *Custard's Last Pie*. They proved that with professional guidance such sensitive writers as John Mason Brown, Alec Woollcott, George Jean Nathan, Percy Hammond, Burns Mantle, and Gilbert Gabriel could act almost as well as camels.

Russel Crouse had a happy thought for the finale of the *P.-D. G.* As master of ceremonies I announced that although the scheduled entertainment had been completed I hoped the audience would stay a few minutes longer. Backstage was an amateur singing trio from West Virginia heartbroken because their bus had arrived too late to let them meet Jack Benny. Would the audience allow them to appear for a moment and take home with them the consolation of having sung in a New York theater? There was approving applause. So three little hillbillies dressed for a trip down the mountain were easily identified as Lily Pons, Gladys Swarthout, and Helen Jepson, queens of the Metropolitan Opera Company. As if they'd been grinding it out all their lives they went to town with a gritty, gut-bucket rendition of "Minnie the Moocher" backed by Duke Ellington's band. They had to bat out so many en-cores we began to wonder if the audience could be driven out of the theater with fire hoses.

I had wanted Charlie Butterworth to repeat his ear-lier success with Phil Baker, not knowing he could not come because of a movie commitment. Instead of saying so he sent me a telegram:

> I refuse to be in the Post-Depression Gaieties. Further-more I don't wish ever to see you again. If you have the gall ever to return to California you will face charges before the Butterworth Athletic Club. I have discovered that between seven and nine dollars are missing from the club treasury. Your fingerprints are all over the shoebox.

I relayed Charlie's telegram to Harry Ruby, saying I was stung to the quick and demanding that Butterworth be made to retract his charges. The next day I received the following from Harry:

> Butterworth was brought before the board of trustees last night. Under torture he confessed he stole the missing money to buy the baseball equipment he was too cheap to pay for out of his own pocket. He was immediately expelled from the club which was thereupon renamed. It is now the *Stay As Sweet As You Are Athletic Club*.

When I next went to Hollywood, Charlie's house was crowded with friends celebrating his birthday. One of the presents he received was an old, swayback horse. When it was led into his living room Charlie exclaimed: "You fel-lows have been reading my mind!"

The success of talkies during the Depression almost killed the living American theater. By 1932, there were fourteen thousand movie houses now wired for sound. The hundreds of legitimate theaters were unable to survive the competition. People hungry for diversion, when offered comfortable seats in picture houses for twenty-five cents forwent paying ten times that much to sit in the decrepit seats of moldy theaters to watch living actors. In New York the theater maintained itself, but only outstanding successes were able to tour the country profitably. *The Green Pastures* was one of them. When Franklin D. Roosevelt pulled America back from the brink of a financial abyss by closing all banks, the immediate shortage of cash was offset by credit buying. Until the moratorium ended, people used checks and I.O.U.'s in place of currency. *The Green Pastures* survived the money shortage amazingly well. When the banks reopened, every check that had been accepted by box offices proved valid, and of the hundreds of small I.O.U.'s, only one failed to be redeemed.

The distress of thousands of men and women dependent on the theater for their livelihood was acute. Hollywood was producing five hundred pictures a year, but the studios offered employment to only a fraction of the twenty-two thousand actors registered with the casting bureaus. Most found only occasional jobs as extras, averaging seventy days of work a year. Almost thirty-thousand musicians had been replaced by mechanical sound. As stock companies virtually disappeared, the mass of stagehands and technicians could find no work. Vaudeville theaters were gone. Between 1930 and 1933, the thirty-six Loew's movie houses that had every year provided between forty and fifty weeks of employment for singers and variety turns had dwindled to three.

In New York, America's theatrical capital, the situation was acute. The relief machinery of the Actors Equity Association was swamped with appeals for aid. Jane Cowl, Rachel Crothers, John Golden, and a half-dozen more of us set up the Stage Relief Fund to meet the needs of the most urgent cases. Frank Case gave us a suite of rooms in the Algonquin to use as offices. Month after month we tried to provide medicine, food, and rent money.

One day an emergency meeting was called to consider an unusual offer of help from a tall, gangling Virginian named Robert Porterfield.

"There's never been a theater in Abington," he said. "I'd like to start one in a barn on my farm. If you get me a mess of actors and a crew to put up a stage I'll feed and house them. I can't pay salaries because nobody in my district has money. But as most of our audiences would be farmers they'd be able to pay for tickets with produce. What do you think?"

"How big a mess do you want?" we asked.

That night twenty-five people were bound for Abington on the truck Porterfield had thoughtfully brought along. The Barter Theater opened two weeks later, and the produce that came over the box office kept the backstage personnel well fed for months. One night a man asked how much milk would get him a seat. He was told one quart. Porterfield, standing in the lobby, watched the farmer join a woman standing beside a cow. He filled a quart pail, brought it to the box office, and received a ticket.

"Don't you want your wife to see the show?" Porterfield asked.

"She can if she wants to," said the farmer. "Give me the pail back and she can milk her own ticket."

When the Empire Theater in New York closed its doors forever in 1953, Porterfield received a bread-cast-on-the-waters sequel to his Depression enterprise. He was told that the Barter Theater, now the partly subsidized State Theater of Virginia, could have virtually all the Empire's furnishings, except for a few of its chairs, which had been given to Howard Lindsay and Russel Crouse, the authors of *Life With Father* which ran longer than any other tenant in the theater's long history.

The next morning a swarm of ex-Barter actors descended on the Empire, and everything was on its way to Abington within a few hours.

One of the brightest days in the history of the American theater dawned in 1935 when the Federal Theater Project of the Works Progress Administration, the W.P.A., came into being. One of the darkest days arrived four years later when an act of Congress killed it. In the meantime, under the leadership of Hallie Flanagan, more than a thousand productions of modern, classical, musical, and children's plays were produced in scores of the country's principal cities.

Many plays pushed back the frontiers of puritanical restrictions. Some did it so vigorously that frightened members of the House Un-American Activities Committee saw Communist propaganda and general subversion in every production that reflected a healthy, liberal view-point on American life. Representatives Martin Dies and J. Parnell Thomas—Thomas later went to jail for payroll padding—spearheaded the fatal congressional attack.

While it lasted, the Federal Theater reversed the tra-ditional economics of play production. As its fundamental purpose was to create jobs, meritorious plays calling for large casts and lots of scenery were favored. Of the many I saw, none gave me more pleasure than *Horse Eats Hat*, an adaptation by Orson Welles and Edwin Denby of Labiche's classic farce *Un Chapeau de Paille d'Italie*. It is one of the few musical plays I can recall vividly. I remem-ber not only *Horse Eats Hat* itself, but the odd circum-stance that in a large attending audience one night at the Maxine Elliott Theater on Thirty-ninth Street only two in-dividuals audibly enjoyed its performance.

I had gone to see it alone. From the moment the cur-tain rose I found it hilarious. So did someone else seated some distance from me whom I couldn't see. We were volcanic islets of mirth in a sea of silence. Hearing another man laughing as much as I was kept me from being intim-idated by the general apathy.

The last scene of the first act was a ballroom in a Paris mansion. It was crowded with guests waltzing to the music of an improbably large band of zimbalon players augmenting the conventional orchestra in the pit. The dancers floated around a fountain playing in the center of the ballroom. (You must remember another object of the Federal Theater was to provide jobs for technicians.) The fugitive hero of the piece, played by the young Joseph Cotten, whom we had seen being chased by half the popu-lation of Paris, dashed onto the stage pursued by gendarmes. The dancers and the music stopped as the hero leaped like a gymnast to the branches of a chandelier. As it swung back and forth, pistols were whipped out from full-dress coats and décolleté gowns. Everyone began firing at the young man on the chandelier. Simultaneously the fountain's jet rose higher, drenching the fugitive until the chandelier on an impulse of its own rose like a balloon out of range. While the shooting kept up, ten liveried footmen made their way through the crowd. As the curtain began to fall they announced to the audience with unruffled dignity: "Supper is served." The moment the curtain shut off the scene a lady cornetist in a hussar's uniform appeared in an upper box and offered a virtuoso demonstration of her skill. As the audience and I moved into the lobby I spotted a man wiping tears of pleasure from his eyes. It was my friend John Dos Passos. For our own security, in case the second act proved as funny as the first, we sat in adjacent vacant seats we found in a rear row and for the rest of the evening screamed with laughter together. I was never able to understand the apathy of the rest of the audience.

I had another unusual experience at a Federal Theater production. It occurred at the Lafayette Theater in Harlem. I had gone there to see William DuBois's *Haiti*, a stirring drama based on the French expulsion of Jean Christophe from his Negro kingdom. The last scene was in the Cap-Haïtien residence of the routed French governor, Le Clerc. The stage was empty, Le Clerc and his household staff having fled to a ship in the harbor. In the distance one heard the yells of Christophe's approaching army, eager to burn the house and kill its occupants. Their actual arrival would have been anticlimactic, so the curtain fell on a swelling volume of sound as they neared the abandoned mansion.

When the cast came onstage for its curtain calls the offstage noises incongruously continued and grew even louder. The houselights went up, and the increasing din suddenly became a roar. The doors to the street had been opened and we had to fight our way to the sidewalk. It turned out to be the very moment all Harlem was learning that Joe Louis had knocked out Max Schmeling.

Another play in which I had a special interest was Thornton Wilder's *Our Town*. The day after its first performance anywhere those interested in its future wondered if they had lost their minds. They had believed the play to be a fresh and beautiful creation. Evidently the Boston public didn't. At the premiere Mrs. Alvan Fuller, the wife of Massachusetts' governor, had walked out during the performance. So had several others in the audience. The reviews of the play in the morning and afternoon newspapers were very discouraging.

Jed Harris had done his magical best to make Wilder's challenging script come alive on the stage. It had been difficult to try to communicate man's place in the universe by means of seemingly random scenes of everyday life in a New Hampshire town and comments by a stage manager who now and then wandered on from the wings and spoke directly to the audience. Even more unusual was the challenge to the audience to imagine most of the scenery. In one scene, for instance, it was asked to believe that two characters were speaking from second-story windows in their homes while actually talking from the upper rungs of ordinary stepladders.

The Monday night opening had been attended by news of a tragic accident. Weeks of grueling rehearsals had brought about the nervous breakdown of Rosamond Pinchot, Jed's production assistant. After the Saturday night dress rehearsal she had gone to her Long Island home for a rest. The next morning she was found in a car in her garage, dead from carbon monoxide. Racked by grief and sleeplessness, Jed had kept himself going on Benzedrine.

The Tuesday and Wednesday audiences had been as unmoved as the first-nighters. Thursday, Jed wondered whether or not to cancel his lease of the Henry Miller Theater in New York, where the play was scheduled to open in ten days. He needed someone to talk to.

I was in New York. Over the telephone he asked me to come up and see that night's performance. I boarded the 5 P.M. train. I got to the Wilbur a few minutes after nine. Jed had had no compunction holding the curtain for me. The handful of people in the audience had brought less than a hundred dollars to the box office. The attendance prospect for Friday and Saturday was so poor that what was to have been a two weeks' engagement had been reduced to one. That afternoon another cloud had been added to the general gloom. Tom Bodkin, Jed's company manager, had slipped on an icy sidewalk and broken a leg.

Backstage the cast was dejected, convinced that *Our Town* would expire after three more performances. Nevertheless the spirited playing of the first act was in the best tradition of the theater.

Despite the first act's fine performance at the Wilbur the audience about me was bewildered. I listened to the entr'acte comment in the lobby. Oh, yes, Frank Craven,

the star, was a fine actor, and this new ingénue Martha
Scott was lovely and talented. But the play—really! The
plot jumped in every direction and went back and forth in
time every which way. What little story it had to tell was
forever being interrupted by Craven's coming out and
talking to the audience. And except for a couple of grape
arbors and some chairs and stepladders brought on after
the play started, there was nothing to see except the theater's steam pipes on the back wall of the stage. They said
that the critics had certainly been right in panning it.

After the performance Jed, Thornton, and I gathered
in Jed's hotel suite. Thornton was as exhausted as Jed.
When we began to talk about the play Thornton was unable to respond to my enthusiasm. "I'm sorry, but my
brain won't function after eleven." As he left, Jed bade
him good night with a caustic, "All right, go to bed, you
god-damned schoolteacher"—a reference to Thornton's
French years as an English master at Lawrenceville.

Jed brightened a bit when I assured him I had found
the play utterly delightful. I like to think that my encouragement helped him decide to bring the play to New
York, but knowing Jed's natural contentiousness, it may
be that my opinions were gratuitous.

Despite his many earlier successes, Jed had been unable to book the Henry Miller for more than ten days,
Gilbert Miller, its owner, having committed it after that
period to another new production.

The day after *Our Town* opened, without a word
changed, the accolades from all the critics made it suddenly desirable to every theater owner in New York with
a faltering tenant. The play received that year's Pulitzer
Prize. Today it is a modern classic, performed thousands

of times annually by professional and amateur companies across the globe.

Since that Thursday evening in Boston, I have been privileged to observe the effect of *Our Town* on many audiences. In 1945 Jed directed a revival of the play in New York's City Center Theater. As Frank Craven was in a movie in California, Jed invited me to play his role. Martha Scott again played Emily and with others of the original cast repeated the success of the earlier production. My performance of the stage manager proved acceptable, and the following year Jed invited me to play the part in London. An exchange had been arranged with the British Arts Council by which Laurence Olivier and others in the Old Vic Company would appear in New York while *Our Town* visited England. While most of the London critics received the play cordially, one or two, like its first audiences in Boston, found it puzzling and indigestible. Happily, the British theatergoers did not share the minority opinion. Most of them arrived at the theater informed of the play's unusual form of presentation and were not confused when taking their seats to discover the curtain already up, on a dark, empty stage.

With the years of war still weighing on their minds Londoners eagerly embraced the mood of the play. Perhaps not so ardently as a man in a California mining town, who was so disturbed by a stage villain's advances on a virtuous heroine that he whipped out a gun and shot the scoundrel dead; but certainly, the Londoners responded in one instance, with the same sense of participation: At the conclusion of a talk on village conditions between the Grover's Corners, New Hampshire, editor and the stage manager, the latter invites the audience to ask questions of their own. The play's script then provides seemingly spontaneous responses from three actors seated widely apart in the audience. One matinee, the actor playing Mr. Webb had "answered" the third inquiry from the other side of the footlights and I was about to speak the next line when we were startled by a fourth question being asked by a *bona fide* theatergoer. She wanted to know if *Our Town* had a public library. I assured her, in a speech Thornton Wilder did not provide, that there was an excellent small library, open daily from 9 A. M. to 9 P. M.. Somehow Editor Webb and I got back into the written dialogue so smoothly that the rest of the audience accepted the impromptu question and its answer as part of the play.

Once, in New York a member of the audience even joined me on the stage. It was at the beginning of the play when the stage manager brings half a dozen chairs from the wings and arranges them to indicate the positions of buildings and streets. As is customary when performances are not in progress, a "pilot light," an electric bulb attached to an upright, movable stand, furnished the only light on the stage. As the audience watched my leisurely procedure a man rose from his seat, climbed the stairs to the stage, and with quiet, friendly concern said that the pilot light was just above his seat and would be in his eyes when the play began. I told him that when I left the stage I would take the light with me. He thanked me and went back to his seat. I doubt that anyone in the audience seeing *Our Town* for the first time was puzzled for a moment by his action.

It is hard to record, in the order of their merit, the many outstanding individual stage performances I have seen. I know that back in the twenties everyone who saw it judged John Barrymore's *Hamlet* to be unforgettable. Great though it was, I found his *Richard III* even more impressive. Barrymore's sinister, half-mad hunchback became incandescent as he gleefully anticipated his conquest of the Lady Anne. The genius of the actor contrived a slight but inspired alteration of Shakespeare's:

Was ever woman in this humour wooed? Was ever woman in this humour won?"

The change to

Never was woman in this manner wooed; never was woman in this manner won.

heightened the deviltry in Richard's gloating.

No single speech ever moved me as deeply as the final moment of Georg Buchner's *Woyzeck* when I saw it some years ago at the exquisite *Teatro Fenice* in Venice. The performance was given by the visiting Kleineschausspielhaus troupe from Munich. Hans Christian Brecht played the tragic, vegetable-like soldier-servant who is plunged into reasonless darkness when he learns that one of his lieutenants has ravished his pretty wife. Almost mechanically he reacts by killing her. He leads the police to the spot where she died. His captors ask what caused him to take her life. For a dramatically long moment Brecht's *Woyzeck* stared at the ground in dumb bewilderment. One almost *saw* the question entering his consciousness. Then his haunted eyes turned to the sky. Mutely, he sought an answer there but failed to find it. He was still seeking it as the curtain slowly descended on the anguish of a crucifixion.

This century has produced no greater American actress than Laurette Taylor. She and her playwright husband, J. Hartley Manners, made the Sunday night suppers at their house on Riverside Drive fantastically gay by charades and other entertainments in which Laurette would spontaneously create characters for improvised playlets. Her artistry was so delicious that the fun of absurd situations and clever acting by others in the game became pale in the blazing light of Laurette's contributions. One night she and the talented actor-playwright Geoffrey Kerr mined gold from a skit Geoffrey had written. It was a scene from an imaginary play and was played three times under different conditions. First we saw it as it might be acted by co-stars, each trying to upstage the other with great finesse. Next we saw it with the actor the star and the actress a "second lead." The third performance cast the actress as the star, hogging the stage while the actor's ego fought for its life. Laurette and Geoffrey not only performed consummately but gave a clinical revelation of what makes actors tick.

In the theater, Laurette glowed in parts that ran from triumphs of buffoon comedy to tragic realism. Perhaps her finest moment was in the scene in *The Glass Menagerie* in which her proud, impoverished southern woman solicited magazine subscriptions over a telephone. The desperate hope for an order under her light, breezy chatter with the possible subscriber, justified the play and would have justified any other actress's career.

The mounting crisis in world affairs had the country jittery in 1940. National self-doubt was increasing as

238

American began to wonder how far they might drift into the lassitude permeating Europe. James Boyd, the novelist, was among those who felt we might be drifting to the same paralysis affecting other nations supposedly patriotic and free.

"If we have no notion of the worth of what we have," he wrote, "we cannot know either how much it should be changed or how far we should go in protecting it."

From that concern came a loosely knitted but energetic organization of writers called The Free Company and a project unique in radio entertainment. The Screen Actors' Guild and the American Federation of Radio Artists agreed to allow their members to give their services free for a series of ten original one-hour plays that the Columbia Broadcasting Company would offer the nation on Sunday nights. The members of The Free Company who volunteered to write the plays were William Saroyan, Robert E. Sherwood, James Boyd, Stephen Vincent Benét, Orson Welles, Paul Green, Archibald MacLeish, Maxwell Anderson, Sherwood Anderson, and myself.

Our plays were intended to communicate aspects of the meaning of our country's freedom and to express faith in its democracy. Several dealt with the eight basic freedoms assured to all citizens in the Bill of Rights.

My own contribution was called *The Mole on Lincoln's Cheek* and involved freedom of speech as applied to our school system. It presented the dilemma of the superintendent of an elementary school who had encouraged the use of history textbooks regarded as communistic by a reactionary school board. The idea came from an actual attack on the excellent and impeccable books by Harold

Rugg, which were then required reading in several states and today are used in classrooms across the nation. Like the books in my play, they are frank appraisals of America's past, occasionally citing such innocuous truths as that Washington wore wooden teeth and that John Hancock like almost everyone else in Massachusetts did some smuggling.

In my play the leader of the reactionaries on the board called the books subversive and corruptive. The superintendent cited Santayana's dictum that "those who do not remember the past are condemned to repeat it." He contended that to prepare a child for responsible citizenship he must be given honest history and not an arrangement of eulogies and flowery obituaries under the guise of history. The climax came when Roberts, one of the board members and presumably on the side of the muttonheads, unexpectedly comes to the superintendent's defense. Etheridge, the chief reactionary, has, among other charges, called the histories muck raking. The high point was the following passage:

ROBERTS: Can't you see *you're* the muckraker?

ETHERIDGE: What are you talking about? Just because I'm American enough to—

ROBERTS: Now, wait a minute. You'll have a chance to answer when I get through. These books don't insult and cheapen our great men. You're doing that by implying they weren't big enough to survive a comparison of their faults and virtues. Let me show you what I mean. All our lives we've been used to seeing pictures and statues of Lincoln with a mole on his cheek—right here. And if any painter or sculptor dared show us Lincoln without that mole there ain't anybody over eight years old in America wouldn't say, "Put that mole back. We know it don't make him look like a movie hero. But he didn't happen to be a movie hero. So you put that mole back, because that's the way he *was*. It makes him realer to us. We want him tall and lanky with big knuckles and his pants not pressed." Now we ought to know America just as well as we know Lincoln. And if parts of our history ain't pretty to look at, let's face the facts and then make improvement as we get the chance to. Want to see what happens to a country filled with little tin gods? Look at Germany. School children there are being taught by your system. All their leaders are perfect and all their histories are being rewritten to prove it. Well, do you want *our* kids to be told about America that way? We know that, every thing considered, it's one of the best countries ever organized. And we want to keep it that way. And that means not being afraid to learn what made it tick in the beginning and what keeps it going today. Now it's getting late and there's a question before the board. But if you ain't convinced yet I'm prepared to sit here all night to get it through that skull of yours.

Melvyn Douglas, Claire Trevor, Edward Ellis, Margaret Hamilton, and Charles Bickford played *The Mole on Lincoln's Cheek* beautifully and, I thought, convincingly. Unhappily William Randolph Hearst saw it as communist propaganda. He aroused at least one California American Legion Post to charge that it slandered Lincoln's memory and demanded that the Columbia broadcastings be stopped. They were—after the tenth and concluding play, Sherwood Anderson's *Above Suspicion*, had been given.

I made no effort to counteract the Hearst charge. Nor did any other member of our group. One reason was that we had all been asked not to disclose the identity of the initiator of The Free Company. It had been feared that the plays might seem like paternal didacticism if it were generally known that it was the U.S. State Department and that its most active representative in working with the organization was Francis Biddle, Solicitor General of the United States.

Ever since I first read *Under Milk Wood* I have believed that had Dylan Thomas been a responsible steward of his talents he could have become the finest dramatist of his time. Long before it was offered on the professional stage it was performed at a seminar on poetry of the theater at the University of Denver which I conducted one summer. For two weeks thirty graduate students and educators considered plays from Tennyson's self-conscious grandiosities to T. S. Eliot's elusive symbolisms. The career poet is usually ill at ease when writing for the theater. More times than not he seems to be wearing the mask of a slumming eighteenth-century fop. Tennyson was ponderously elegant but an honest workman. His *Queen Mary, Harold, Becket,* and *The Falcon,* like Browning's *The Return of the Druses* and *A Blot on the 'Scutcheon,* were performed by illustrious stars but did not stir audiences used to Shakespeare's employment of the same dramatic forms. The seams of Eliot's *Cocktail Party* frequently rip, exposing the poorness of his dramaturgic needlework and the confusion of his storytelling. To me only his *Murder in the Cathedral* shows valid substance and theatrical realization.

By contrast, Dylan Thomas flashed lightning, and his thunder was not from an offstage metal sheet. The characters and lines of *Under Milk Wood* hardly need actors to give them voice and reality.

I had seen another facet of Dylan Thomas's genius one extraordinary June afternoon in 1945 in London. An audience that included many of Britain's eminent poets had gathered for the Poetry Society's annual "reading" in an Edwardian recital hall in Wigmore Street. After an introduction by John Masefield, the Poet Laureate and president of the Society, the program would start with recitations of early English poetry by Edith Evans, Flora Robson, and John Gielgud. They would be followed by Edith Sitwell, Walter de la Mare, T. S. Eliot, Dylan Thomas, and others, who might or might not read from their own works. As usual, Queen Elizabeth would be present, this time accompanied by her daughters, the Princesses Elizabeth and Margaret Rose.

Thomas, like everyone else, arrived before the royal party. He caused consternation by appearing without a necktie, and a member of the reception committee was dispatched to buy one for him.

St. John Irvine and I had been invited by Dr. Masefield. It was our privilege to sit in the front row of seats with the Queen and her daughters. I found myself beside Princess Elizabeth, then nineteen. Other than my receiving a gracious smile when I was presented, our social contact was limited to her showing me the handsome copy of *The Canterbury Tales* she had been given as a souvenir of the occasion. All I remember of our meeting was her saying: "Isn't it lovely?" and my courtly reply that it certainly was.

Dr. Masefield, in a dark gray morning jacket and striped trousers, started the proceedings. Gravely, like a student speaking before classmates at Fifth Form Declamation, Dr. Masefield bowed and began: "My Queen," continuing with a brief rhymed greeting as charming as a Victorian valentine.

The three representatives of the theater provided the

first half of the program. When Flora Robson finished the trio's stint there were tea and cakes backstage. The Queen and the Princesses conversed with the actors and the poets who were to appear next. Thomas, wearing a tie, dutifully thanked the Queen for her compliments.

The second part was begun by the aging Walter de la Mare. He read two poems from *Peacock Pie*. His quavering, musical voice filled the air with butterflies.

I had previously watched Edith Sitwell three or four times when she had been as much actress as poet, offering what were more performances than recitals. Today she was evidently all set to act again. Had her velvety costume been red it might have served someone playing Cardinal Richelieu. She seemed to feel a spotlight about her and to enjoy the flections of her voice as much as, if not more than, her audience.

When T. S. Eliot rose to follow her I hoped he would recite something from *Old Possum's Book of Practical Cats*, which I irreverently value more than his profundities. Instead he had chosen a humorless selection. His platform manner was stiff and somber. I closed my eyes. The slightly stressed cadences of relentlessly long stanzas made me hear Cotton Mather droning in his pulpit.

I am ashamed I have forgotten the name of the Scottish poet who followed Eliot. He had none of his predecessor's solemnity, and his voice was as refreshing as spring rain. He forwent offering anything he had written. Instead he transported us to a highland brae with Robert Burns, and we smelled heather.

Whoever arranged the program had been inspired in placing Dylan Thomas last. He walked to the center of the stage with easy grace. After standing silently for a moment he recited, slowly and quietly, the beginning of a poem usually ascribed to William Blake. He murmured, "Tiger! tiger! burning bright—" Then in less time than you could have waved a wand magic took over Wigmore Hall. The sound of the words we were hearing increased in volume, but now they were not being spoken by a man standing before us on a platform. We were no longer conscious of Dylan Thomas or aware of our physical surroundings. Only our ears were functioning. They were hearing an incredibly lovely poem come into existence. If the sounds of the forests of the night were issuing from any throat it was Merlin's, carrying from a thornbush in Wales.

As one of the guests of honor I had been asked to stay for the departure of the royal party. The palace limousines had been parked inconspicuously in a short, narrow street behind the hall. Their presence had collected a cluster of young girls from nearby shops and offices, who made a little aisle as the Queen's group moved to the automobiles. After their doors were closed there was a brief delay in starting. During the wait the girls pressed close to the windows of the car containing the Queen. Several young hands fluttered affectionately as if before the glass wall of a maternity ward nursery. Queen Elizabeth, with a smile as warm as any being given her, kept waving back until she was borne away.

Dr. Masefield asked me my reaction to the reading. I truthfully said it had been one of the most delightful experiences of my life.

"Were you surprised by the Queen's interest in poetry?" he asked. I said I was, as it had been my impression that British royal tastes in entertainment usually ran to less intellectual pleasures.

"Not Her Majesty's. Let me assure you that the Queen is not only very fond of poetry but that she reads a great deal of philosophy." The eyes of England's Poet Laureate twinkled. He glanced to his right, then to his left, as though great caution must be exercised before anything more was said. Then in a half whisper he confided: "Of course she was not *born* royal."

The first time I met the Queen Mum was in the early thirties when she was the young and captivating Duchess of York. She was a close friend of Lady Leamington, the sister of my friend William Post, Mayor LaGuardia's Commissioner of Housing. Whenever the former Mary Post entertained Americans in her Belgrave Mansion, the Duchess was informed. She liked Americans and, if she had the time, was usually on hand when they arrived.

Mary had invited my wife and me to cocktails. We found ourselves interjecting conversational "Ma'ams" as we sat beside the Duchess, a short, very attractive woman wearing a light gray dress and a light gray hat. The Duchess asked me how we had spent the day and I reported that we had just come from a visit to London Tower. She asked me to tell her about it. I tried to be amusing in describing the Beefeater guide who had all the patience in the world for the visitors arriving after he had begun his routine speech.

I hoped to amuse the Duchess by an imitation of the guide's Seven Dials' pronunciation.

"Kindly step this w'y, please. You are now standing in what is known as the Bloody Tower. The nyme comes from what 'appened to prisoners sent 'ere by Lord Chancellor George Jeffreys, 'oose own nyme is branded with infamy. In sixteen eyeghty-five Judge Jeffreys reeked 'is fury on Titus Hoates, 'oo 'ad been involved in the Rye 'Ouse plot and 'oo— Come right in please. I was just beginning to explyne 'ow the Bloody Tower got its nyme. It comes from what 'appened to prisoners sent 'ere by Lord Chancellor George Jeffreys, 'oose own nyme is branded with infamy. In sixteen eyeghty-five— Come right in please. We're just getting underw'y. I was s'ying this is called the Bloody Tower. The nyme comes from what 'appened . . ."

The Duchess was a responsive audience. Her laughter spurred me to report more of the afternoon's incidents. She seemed to be fascinated. Whenever I paused she asked another question, and I tried to answer entertainingly. After a while her eyes left mine for a moment as if in contemplation. Suddenly a chastening thought struck me. Instead of entertaining her had I been trying the patience of a bored listener too gracious and gentle to tell me I had talked too much?

I was about to end her duress when she again questioned me. She asked about the dimensions and appearance of the Jewel Tower. As I replied, another thought hit me. I remembered that the City of London in which the Tower is situated is rarely visited by British royalty and then only at the invitation of the City's Lord Mayor.

"Ma'am," I said, "let me ask you something. Have you ever seen the Tower?"

"No," said the Duchess, rather plaintively. "And I don't recall ever having talked with anyone who had been there."

Most of England was still eating rationed gray bread and powdered eggs in the summer of 1945, but London was bouncing with postwar festivity. The "illuminations" had brought throngs to see the capital once again relighted after nearly five years of darkness. One night I watched a young father lift his three-year-old daughter above the sea of heads on the Mall. Tears ran down his cheeks when he heard her squeals of delight as she watched a comparatively meager cluster of colored lights playing on a single fountain across the road in St. James's Park.

The Duke of Edinburgh was then simply Prince Philip and about the best-liked young man in London. His popularity had very little to do with his royal Greek lineage or his being the nephew of England's illustrious army commander, the Earl of Mountbatten. People liked him because he was intelligent, witty, and lighthearted, as gay and stimulating a companion as anyone could ever hope to meet.

For several weeks I encountered him almost nightly at parties. It was not long before we had a first-name acquainceship. One midnight as I was leaving an after-theater dance, Philip casually asked if he would see me at a party someone was giving the next night. I said I couldn't go because the following morning I was leaving for Sweden to be a delegate from the American P.E.N. Center to the first international Congress since the start of the war.

"The meeting will be in Stockholm?"

I said it would.

"Then you must say hello to my aunt."

Among the books I have never read is Debrett's *Peerage*. Therefore, I innocently replied, "I'll be glad to, if I meet her, but I don't know who she is."

Philip exploded with laughter. "She's the Crown Princess, you dope."

A week or so later the P.E.N. delegates were guests for tea at the Royal Palace. When I met Sweden's future Queen Louise, I facetiously remarked that I had come with some instructions from her nephew.

"From Philip?" Her look implied a slight bewilderment.

"Yes, ma'am. He said I should say hello to you."

It was only a split second before Princess Louise demonstrated that she enjoyed nonsense as much as Philip did.

"I see." Sweden's future queen chuckled. "Please tell him I am deeply grateful."

Prince William was president of the Swedish P.E.N. chapter, our official host, and the hospitality offered the two hundred delegates from Europe and the Americas was endless. I had flown up from London with Desmond MacCarthy, the president of the English P.E.N. and dean of British literary and dramatic critics. He had never been in a plane before, but he was the only calm passenger in ours when an unexpected turbulence dropped our plane several hundred feet and caused a terrifying crash. It seemed to come from the rear section of the plane. Mr. MacCarthy turned toward me, smiling, his confidence in the plane's stability unruffled. He obviously expected me, the veteran flyer, to explain what had nearly every passenger white as a sheet. I rose and looked to the rear. The blood came back to my cheeks when I saw a stewardess gazing in despair at a great trayload of cups, saucers, and plates lying shattered on the floor.

Phyllis Bottome and another lady novelist were among the English delegates. We were quartered in the

Hotel Eden and had dinner together on the evening of our arrival. Swedish food is always excellent, and we ate heartily. The next day all the English delegates were ill. Miss Bottome and several others were so badly stricken they had to spend the next two days in bed. Their doctors' diagnosis was that their stomachs had violently resisted the good butter and other edibles they had been denied for thousands of meals.

The Danes are among my favorite people. One of their delegates at the Congress was the playwright Kjeld Abell. Besides being a brilliant craftsman, he was a national hero, one of the leaders of the underground who had harassed the Germans from the moment they had occupied Denmark. It was Abell who risked his life to tell his countrymen of the death of the clergyman-dramatist Kaj Munk, a daring and popular spokesman for the Resistance. Kaj Munk was seized by the Germans early in January, 1944, murdered, and left in a ditch not far from his vicarage on the west coast of Jutland. To weaken Danish morale a report was immediately circulated that he had been killed by the underground for betraying its activities. The day after his death all Denmark was shocked by the report. That night a large audience that included scores of German officers was watching a play in Copenhagen's opera house. In the middle of a scene Abell calmly walked down an aisle, climbed onto the stage, and halted the gasps of astonishment by shouting:

"They are telling you we killed him. They lie. We loved him. They did it!"

There must have been Nazis in the audience who recognized him, but before he could be seized, he had dashed backstage and escaped.

During the Stockholm Congress, Abell was one of the

guests at a dinner at Manilla, the great town house of the Bonnier family in Djurgården. About fifty of the delegates were present, guests of Fru Lisen Bonnier, the elderly matriarch head of the Bonnier publishing empire whose magazines, newspapers, and books circulate throughout Scandinavia. It was a gala occasion. The brightness of the conversation over delicious wines and food somewhat lightened the hearts of men and women in mourning for their losses in the war.

It is a long-established custom at formal Swedish dinners for guests to interrupt general conversation by offering toasts and brief comments. They invariably consume less than thirty seconds each and usually fillip the enjoyment of the occasion. The most eloquent toast I ever heard was made that night by Kjeld Abell. He rose and tapped a glass. Addressing our frail eighty-three-year-old hostess he said:

"Sweden! I am enjoying the first food and drink I have tasted on your soil since the day my country was invaded. But never during our long separation were we Danes without nourishment from you. You constantly fed us life-sustaining help and friendship. And on our darkest nights we had only to look across the water to the lights of Malmö and they gave us warmth!"

It has long been a rule that what happens in a gentlemen's club must never be mentioned in public. The Players Club has always been an exception. It is so rich with tradition that its members have always felt free to tell the outside world about the personalities and activities that have brightened the graceful old building at 16 Gramercy Park on New York's east side. Edwin Booth retained a small apartment in it when in 1888 he presented it to the club he had organized with John Drew, Brander Matthews, Joseph Jefferson, Mark Twain, Thomas Bailey Aldrich, General William Tecumseh Sherman, Lawrence Barrett, and other friends. As its name implies, it is primarily an actors' club, but its membership has always included representatives of all the arts.

I first entered its doors in my early twenties. I was barely earning a living and grateful for the friendship of Fred Erving Dayton and Helena Smith Dayton, his wife. Fred edited a trade magazine and wrote an engrossing definitive history of Mississippi riverboats. Helena was a successful painter and sculptress. In the teens and twenties their house in Greenwich Village was a haven for fellow artists.

The day Fred introduced me to the Players, we had lunch on the veranda, which enclosed a tiny garden in the center of which a little fountain played. We had a wonderful dessert that day. It was a custard pie so delicious that I promised myself that if I ever had the luck to become a Player I would order that marvelous pie whenever I could. Happily I became a member in 1922, but for almost half a century I have looked in vain for custard pie to appear on the club's menu.

I doubt that any club has produced as much good conversation and fun as The Players. Numberless witticisms first uttered there are part of America's treasury of humor. Here are some I don't believe have ever been made public before:

One night Moffat Johnson was in a group at the bar listening to a fellow Player fervidly moralizing on a murder case then filling the newspapers. A Hawaiian beach boy had been killed by an American naval officer. The officer's defense was that the boy had raped his wife. Moffat was an eminent actor noted for his precise English speech. He was really a Scot and often after a few relaxing highballs would fall back on the dialect of his childhood densely thick with burrs. Moffat nodded approvingly as the speaker argued that the tragedy was another instance of the havoc that invariably followed the imposition of the white man's standards of morality on primitive cultures.

"That beachboy was the victim of our civilization, the inevitable result of the white man's forcing his rules of life on Hawaiians. He brought hypocrisy, greed, moral collapse, and every other kind of degradation to a gentle, harmless, contented people."

Moffat took a meditative swig and said, "Aye, there's a greet muckle of truth in what ye say aboot the white man. He domn near ruined Scotland."

Oliver Herford was an inexhaustible source of pithy remarks. Nearly everything he said evoked laughter. Once he made an observation that wasn't funny. It sprang from his heart when he observed a customary black-bordered card on the bulletin board announcing the death of another member. He spoke softly to the crony standing beside him:

"Always the wrong man."

I have been the luckiest of men in encountering people who have enriched my life, either by their personalities or their achievements. I knew William Butler Yeats, James Stephens, Lennox Robinson, Oliver St. John Gogarty,

George Russell, whose pseudonym was A.E., Lord Dunsany, Bernard Shaw and other Irishmen and am grateful for the wisdom and gaiety that sprang from their lips. I have heard each of them tell revealing anecdotes about the others. Gogarty, a most enthralling storyteller, used to hold me by the hour remembering Yeats's odd displays of humor.

"One night Yeats was on a steamer crossing the Irish Sea," Gogarty once told me. "He was standing on deck enjoying a furious storm which was tossing everyone about. A young English girl made her way to the ship's rail beside him. She mistook Yeats's long black cloak and somewhat clerical hat as those of a clergyman.

" 'Father,' she said earnestly, 'I'm badly frightened. Would you say a prayer for me?'

"Of course Yeats hadn't been in a church for years and years. But he wanted to give the girl solace. He lifted his eyes piously, and on the premise that the English regarded Milton at least on a parity with the King James version of the Bible, he shouted above the wind:

> Hence, vain deluding Joys,
> The brood of Folly without father bred!
> How little you bested,
> Or fill the fixed mind with all your toys!

"When he finished, the girl stared at him, confused but grateful. Yeats contended his effort proved the power of great poetry, because the storm stopped before he'd finished."

Yeats was a man who knew when he was licked in a verbal set-to. After one of his lectures an eager young thing with shining eyes dashed up to him. Yeats beamed at her, always prepared to accept compliments from pretty girls.

"Oh, Mr. Yeats," this one gurgled. "I *so* enjoyed hearing your poems. Might I dare ask you a question?"

Yeats with lordly grace said she might.

"It's this," said his admirer. "Would you tell why you read everything in such a sing-song manner?"

Yeats was taken back and became a couple of degrees cooler.

"My dear young lady," he said from Olympus, "the rhythm of my speech happens to be one employed by every poet worth his salt since Homer."

The girl seemed grateful. "Oh, I never knew that! How *very* interesting." Then as deferentially as before, she ventured: "Might I ask you another question?"

Still somewhat ruffled, Yeats said of course she could.

"I'm afraid I'm puzzled. Would you tell me by what authority you know Homer read that way?"

Yeats knew he'd met his match and realized he'd better admit it. He surrendered with a grin.

"My authority is that of the Scot who when asked why he persistently declared that Shakespeare had been born in the highlands argued: 'My authority is the outstanding excellence of the man!' "

I once saw Bernard Shaw's aplomb jolted a bit. Mrs. Shaw had invited my wife and me to lunch in the Shaws' London flat. It was in 1932. There were eight of us at the table, my wife, Madeline, at Shaw's right. Mrs. Shaw and her guests were served meat, but Shaw's main course, though it looked like conventional chicken croquettes was, a mixture of peas, potatoes, and nuts, perhaps, under a whitish cream sauce. This soft food had enabled Shaw to do almost all the talking since we arrived, I wondered if I had found a secondary reason for his vegetarianism.

I had long been interested in Shaw's friendship with Gene Tunney. I asked him how it had begun. "You didn't meet Tunney until long after you wrote *Cashel Byron's Profession*," I reminded him. "Have you always had an interest in boxing?"

"Not in boxing alone," Shaw replied. "I've always been curious about people who have a passion for strenuous physical exercise. They seem to believe incessant muscle building of vital importance to their health. They unnerve me a bit."

With the same seeming ingenuousness of Yeats's young heckler my wife broke in.

"Why, Mr. Shaw! Am I to think the only exercises you ever take are walking, swimming, bicycling, tennis, hill climbing, horseback riding, and the other activities we see you constantly doing in our rotogravure sections?"

Mrs. Shaw and the rest of us burst into laughter. And because Shaw, like Yeats, was quicker than most men to laugh at himself he glared at my wife, then turned on the rest of the company with pretended fury.

"And who, may I ask," he demanded, "brought this young woman to my house?"

Epilogue

SEVENTY YEARS have passed since the theater first filled me with wonder and delight. During that time I have enjoyed its blessings and given what I had to give in its service. I cannot claim to have adorned it with anything as lasting as the embellishments of the mediaeval sculptors on the cathedral's face, but I have occasionally tried to brighten its altar with flowers from my garden.

My love for it has grown with my familiarity with its mysteries. Western man began to identify them more than twenty-five hundred years ago. He discovered them in the satyr plays acted before wayside shrines, which invited worshipers to relate themselves to the divinity they honored. The mysteries became clearer when later Greeks built Epidaurus, that sacred place of healing waters. There they constructed a great half-cone in which another kind of therapy could be practiced. The vast theater became a hospital of the spirit. Dramatists supplied invigorating nourishment to the mind. Comedians provided the tonic of laughter.

Down the years the theater has retained its health-giving properties and applied them with its own unique methods. The theater instructs but is not a didactic teacher. If offers suggestions, not statements. It extends invitations to belief without dogmatic insistences. *Drama* means to do. When it operates, the doing is almost entirely the work of the audience. The actor does not laugh at his joke; it becomes a joke only when the audience accepts it as one. The stage is a place for implication, not polemics. It is twisted out of shape when someone tries to make it a lecture platform, a pulpit, or a soapbox. Its ritual is a form of hypnosis, which frees individuals from the constrictions of their identities and personal conditionings. When its chemistry has converted spectators into participants, it offers joys that make the heart leap and conducts explorations that can lead the soul to answers.

The theater must have freedom to function properly. Its reason for being lies in the simple premise that self-knowledge is vital to man's growth. The fears of puritans and insecure autocrats always demand that the theater accept the restraints and patterns of conduct they dare not see questioned. They know that in the theater, social and moral patterns are examined but not preached.

Sometimes the theater's custodians do not bring honest dedication to their stewardship. Playwrights' voices are often too strident and offer less persuasion than clamor. They exploit the theater rather than serve it. And often, as Dryden said, they dress pygmy thoughts in giant words. Comedy is less victimized by disservice. Gaiety is hard to counterfeit, and today's funmakers, true to their lineage, are almost always the humblest of the theater's priesthood and continue to serve it faithfully.

Finally let me say that I believe the theater is the best social instrument man has ever devised. The scope of its observation is limitless. A raindrop, Lord Dunsany once remarked, is small, yet it can reflect the whole sky. And where on earth can one find a finer place in which to seek truth under pleasant circumstances?

A Note on the Type

The text of this book was set on the Linotype in Janson, a recutting made direct from type cast from matrices long thought to have been made by the Dutchman Anton Janson, who was a practicing type founder in Leipzig during the years 1668–87. However, it has been conclusively demonstrated that these types are actually the work of Nicholas Kis (1650–1702), a Hungarian, who most probably learned his trade from the master Dutch type founder Kirk Voskens. The type is an excellent example of the influential and sturdy Dutch types that prevailed in England up to the time William Caslon developed his own incomparable designs from these Dutch faces.

The book was composed, printed, and bound by Vail-Ballou Press, Inc.

Design by Robert Reed.